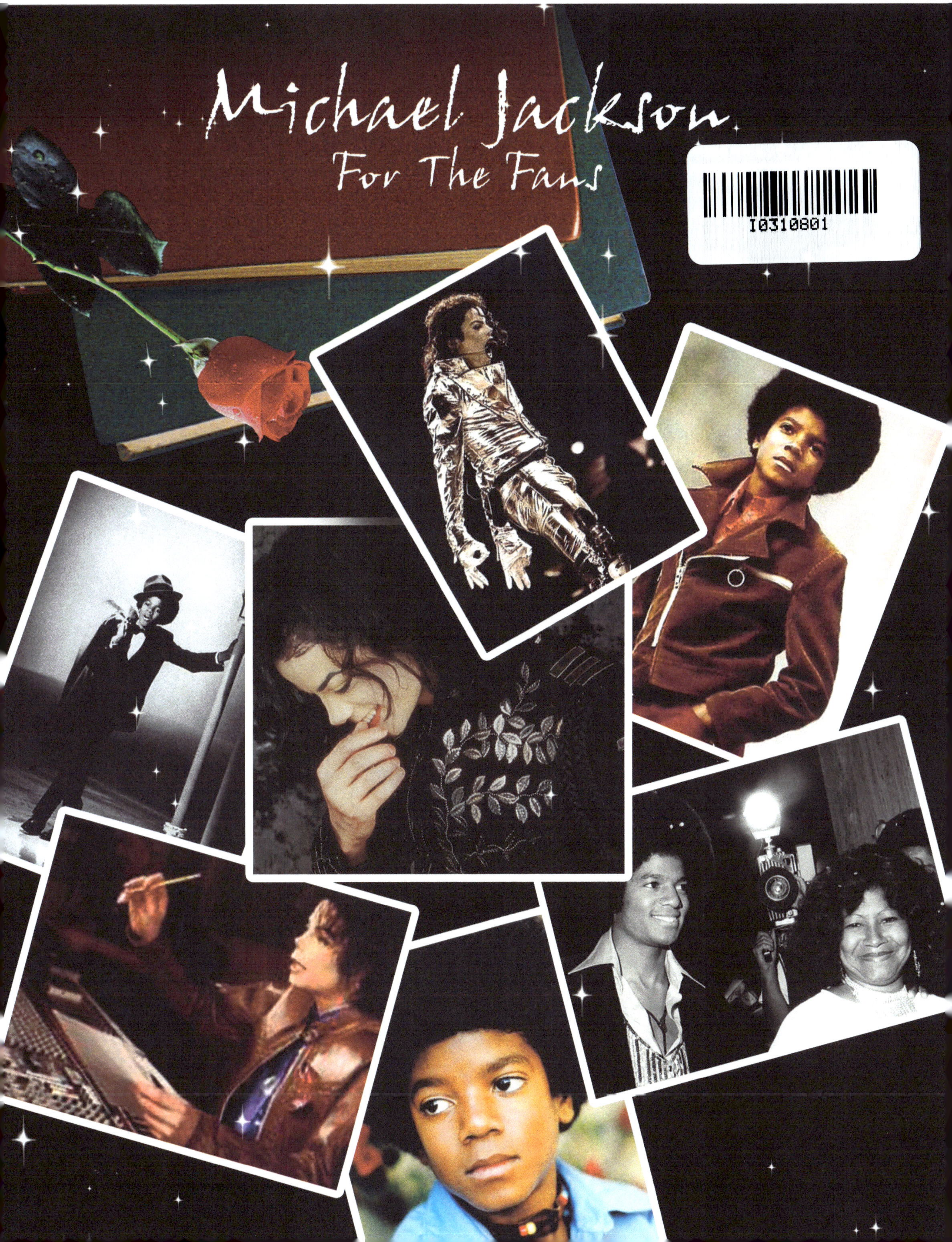

Michael Jackson
For The Fans

FOREWORD

The true essence of a man may only be revealed when he is no longer present to defend himself. For as long as he speaks to preserve his own merit, people will consistently seek to destroy his value. But as soon as his voice is silenced in time his deeds become more apparent, and his significance unsurpassable.

As morbid as it may be, death has a way of articulating to the world what should have been evident in life. It can generate a summation that will detail who we are from the cradle to the grave. It matters not the portrait we want to paint, nor the brush we choose to use. But instead, the true colors that are disclosed is the authentic reflection of what we see when we are looking in the mirror.

Michael Jackson has been said to be by a variation of persons, an icon. He has also been described as "The King of Pop." A vast number of people have even said that the world-renowned celebrity is perhaps the greatest entertainer to have ever lived. But by whatever standards we choose to measure him, he was conceivably one of the most generous, compassionate, and kindest individuals that this world may ever know.

Michael started his contributions at an early age. As the lead vocalist for the group The Jackson 5, Michael gave us all a part of him. When he sang and danced, he made us forget, if only for the duration of the 45 record that was playing, any trials or tribulations that were lurking nearby. Michael moved into most of our homes and became a part of our family. He grew with us, and he became a son, a brother, and in some cases, a boyfriend. When Ed Sullivan brought Michael into our living rooms in 1970 as he and his brothers sang "I want you back", we instantaneously fell in love with him and immediately knew that we could "Never say goodbye." Young Michael Jackson had blown into our lives and taken us by storm, he had become one who would be often

FOREWORD

For the next several years Michael Jackson and the Jackson 5 would enchant America with songs such as ABC, The Love You Save and I'll Be There. Their continued success with tunes like Mama's Pearl, Sugar Daddy and Never Can Say Goodbye swept the United States and show cased the charisma of young Michael Jackson. The Jackson 5 with their lead singer Michael was a smashing sensation. The sons of Joseph and Katherine were undeniably the hottest new R&B group on the charts, and their potential for growth could not be restrained.

As Michael grew, so did the rest of the world. Eventually he left our living rooms and our homes and he moved abroad. He developed a desire to make contributions not only in his native land, but worldwide. It became clear, just by watching this boy wonder that he had big dreams, and high hopes. Michael wasn't content with simply a domestic display of his talent, he wanted to reach out and share with the world the joy that he felt when he was on stage. He wanted to make contributions in lands that his feet had never traveled. Even as a child Michael's commitment to the world was manifest in his actions and performances as he reached out to connect with his audiences.

Michael Jackson was an astounding human being; millions around the world felt his generosity. As Michael became larger than life, so did his heart. He had an insatiable desire to serve those who were less fortunate. Michael had a dream of a world united. He didn't believe that color, financial status, nor ignorance should divide or conquer us. He believed in a world of love, a world where violence could subside and hunger could be healed. With a child's heart, Michael strived daily to do what he could to make this world a more pleasant place to live. Even though he encountered tragedies, and faced many of obstacles, he never allowed defeat to impede his quest for a brighter tomorrow.

FOREWORD

On June 25, 2009, Michael Joseph Jackson transitioned into a world in which we are all destined to travel. He left us a legacy of love that should inspire us to take a look at who we are and then look at the world in which we live and decide how we can make it a better place. As Michael stated in one of his songs, change starts with the man or the woman that you see in the mirror every day. Contrary to what is believed, Michael was right, "We are the world, we are the children. We are the ones who make a brighter day, so let's start giving. There's a choice we're making, we're saving our own lives, it's true we'll make a better day, just you and me." If we don't take anything else away from the death of this legendary icon, known as "The King of Pop, who just happened to be the greatest entertainer to have ever lived, let us remember the love that he shared with us, from the cradle to the grave. Let's remember that he believed in this world and he believed in a force that was strong enough to restore the worst of conditions. He believed that love was the cure to the distress that the world endured.

We salute you Michael: "In a world filled with hate, we must still dare to hope. In a world filled with anger, we must still dare to comfort. In a world filled with despair, we must still dare to dream. And in a world filled with distrust, we must still dare to believe."   - Michael Jackson

August 29, 1958 – June 25, 2009

Michael Jackson

Michael Joseph Jackson (born August 29, 1958) is an American musician and entertainer whose successful music career has been at the forefront of pop culture for the last quarter-century.

Jackson began his musical career at the age of seven as the lead singer of The Jackson 5 and released his first solo recording, Got to Be There in 1971, while remaining a member of the group. He began a full-fledged solo career in 1979 and formally parted with his siblings in 1984. In his solo career, Jackson recorded and co-produced the best-selling album of all time, Thriller, which was named as the world's best-selling album at the 2006 World Music Awards. It has worldwide sales exceeding that of 104 million. Michael Jackson has received thirteen Grammy awards and charted thirteen number-one singles in the United States.

Throughout his four-decade career, Michael Jackson has been awarded numerous honors including the World Music Award's Best-Selling Pop Male Artist of the Millennium, American Music Award's Artist of the Century Award and the Bambi Award's Pop Artist of the Millennium Award. He is a double-inductee of the Rock and Roll Hall of Fame (once as a member of The Jackson 5 in 1997, and as a solo artist in 2001) and an inductee of the Songwriters Hall of Fame.

1966-1980: Early Life & Career

Michael Jackson was born in Gary, Indiana. He is the second-youngest brother of seven and the eighth of ten children of Joseph and Katherine Jackson. In 1966, after taking co-lead singing duties with brother Jermaine, the group's name changed from The Jackson Brothers to The Jackson 5. The group played at local clubs and bars, building up a following and eventually signing a contract with Motown Records in 1968.

The group hit stardom, with their first four singles which charted at number-one on the Billboard Hot 100. As a solo artist, Jackson released Got to Be There in 1971 and Ben in 1972. These were released as part of the Jackson 5 franchise and produced successful singles such as "Got to Be There", "Ben", and a remake of Bobby Day's "Rockin' Robin".

The group's sales declined after 1973 and the group grew irritated that Motown refused to allow the Jacksons creative control or input. In 1976, the group signed a new contract with CBS Records (first joining the Philadelphia International division and then Epic Records). When this became apparent to Motown Records, they sued the group for breach of contract.

Michael Jackson

As a result of the legal proceedings, which were complicated further by the fact that Jermaine Jackson was married to the daughter of Motown president (Berry Gordy), the Jacksons lost the rights to use the "Jackson 5" name and logo and also Jermaine, who wanted to stay at Motown. They changed their name to "The Jacksons", featuring youngest brother Randy in Jermaine's place, and continued their successful career, touring internationally and releasing six more albums between 1976 and 1984, with Jermaine eventually re-joining in 1983, making them a sextet.

In 1978, Michael starred as the scarecrow in The Wiz with former-label mate Diana Ross playing Dorothy. The songs for the musical were arranged by Quincy Jones, who established a partnership with Jackson during the film's production and agreed to produce his first solo album in four years. Off the Wall, released in 1979, was a worldwide hit, and became the first album in history to spawn four top-ten hits, including "Don't Stop 'Til You Get Enough" and "Rock With You".

In January 1980, Jackson won his first awards for his solo efforts at the American Music Awards. He won "Favorite Soul/R&B Album" (for Off The Wall), "Favorite Male Soul/R&B Artist" and Favorite Soul/R&B Single (for "Don't Stop 'Til You Get Enough"). Later that month, he also won two Billboard Awards (for "Black Artist of the Year" and "Top Black Album").

On February 27, 1980, Jackson won a Grammy Award for "Best R&B Vocal Performance, Male" (for "Don't Stop 'Til You Get Enough").

1982–1986: The Thriller era

In November 1982, the storybook for E.T.: The Extra-terrestrial was released. It included Jackson reading the story as well as one original song ("Someone in the Dark"). The album later won a Grammy for "Best Album for Children".

In December 1982, Jackson released his second Epic album, Thriller, which became the best-selling album in music history. The album spawned seven hit singles, including "Billie Jean" (which was the first music video by a black artist to receive regular airplay on MTV), "Beat It" and the album's title track which was accompanied by a revolutionary music video. The thirteen-minute "Thriller" was critically acclaimed and massive airplay lead to it being packaged with the featurette "Making Michael Jackson's "Thriller" on VHS, where it became the best-selling music home video ever.

Michael Jackson

Thriller spent 37 weeks at number-one and remained on the Billboard album chart for 122 weeks. It was eventually certified 27x Platinum in the United States.

In 1983, while performing "Billie Jean" at the Motown 25: Yesterday, Today, Forever concert Jackson debuted what can be regarded as his signature move: the moonwalk. In 1983, he started a sponsorship deal with Pepsi-Cola, and, as part of the deal, he agreed to star in a commercial. While filming a Pepsi commercial with his brothers in 1984, before a live audience, his hair caught on fire when a pyrotechnic effect went wrong. Jackson suffered second-degree burns on his scalp, which required skin grafts.

In February 1984, Jackson is nominated for twelve Grammy awards which he won eight, breaking the record for the most Grammy awards won in a single year. Seven were for the critically acclaimed Thriller and the other for the E.T.: The Extra-terrestrial storybook. In 1984, he also won eight American Music Awards and the "Special Award of Merit" and three MTV Video Music Awards.

After reuniting with his brothers, he helped to write the Victory album. He then performed and starred in the successful Victory Tour which started on July 6, 1984 and lasted for five months.

In 1985, Michael was invited to the White House and was personally thanked by then-President Ronald Reagan at a White House ceremony for donating the song "Beat It" for use in drunk driving prevention television and radio public service announcements.

Jackson continued his charity work in 1985 by co-writing, with Lionel Richie, the hit single "We Are the World". The charity single helped to raise money and awareness for the famine in East Africa and was one of the first instances where Michael was seen as a humanitarian. The song also won a Grammy Award for "Song of the Year".

Also in 1985, Michael showed his business smarts when he purchased shares in the ATV Music Publishing (a company which owned the rights to most of the Beatles' songs), making himself the majority shareholder. In 1986, Jackson starred in the George Lucas-produced, Francis Ford Coppola directed 3-D film Captain EO. The film lasted 17 minutes but had costs estimated at $17 million.

Michael Jackson

At the time, it was the most expensive film ever produced on a per-minute basis. In the USA, the Disney theme parks hosted Captain EO. Disneyland featured the film in tomorrow-land from September 18, 1986 until April 7, 1997. It was also featured in Walt Disney World in Epcot from September 12, 1986 until July 6, 1994.

1987–1990: Bad Era

In 1987, Jackson released Bad; his third album for the Epic record label, and final album with producer Quincy Jones. He initially wanted to make the album 30 tracks long, but Jones cut this down to 10.

In comparison to Thriller, Bad had lower sales but it was still a huge commercial success. It spawned seven hit singles, of which five went to number-one, those being: "I Just Can't Stop Loving You", "Bad", "The Way You Make Me Feel", "Man in the Mirror", and "Dirty Diana". The album went onto sell 29 million copies worldwide; the Recording Industry Association of America eventually certified Bad at 8x Platinum. In September 1987, he embarked upon his first solo world tour, the Bad World Tour. The tour lasted sixteen months, in which Jackson performed at 123 concerts, to over 4.4 million fans worldwide. Jackson insisted on a personal bus, plane and helicopter to be available to him all at the same time.

Jackson hired film director Martin Scorsese to direct the video for the album's title track.

The success Jackson achieved during this period in his career led to him to be dubbed the "King of Pop", a nickname which he continues to be referred to by fans. There are various conflicting reports as to the origin of the nickname. According to Jackson, it was conceived by actress and long-term friend Elizabeth Taylor when she presented Jackson with an "Artist of the Decade" award in 1989, proclaiming him "the true king of pop, rock and soul". Additionally, this period saw Jackson enjoy "a level of superstardom previously known only to Elvis Presley, the Beatles and Frank Sinatra".

1991–1994: Dangerous and further career

In March 1991, Michael Jackson renewed his contract with Sony for $65 million, a record-breaking deal at the time, displacing Neil Diamond's renewal contract with Columbia Records.

Michael Jackson

In November 1991, Michael Jackson released Dangerous. The album's first single "Black or White" was its biggest hit, reaching number one on the Billboard Hot 100 and remaining there for seven weeks, with similar chart performances worldwide. The album's second single "Remember the Time" spent eight weeks in the top five in the United States, peaking at number three on the Billboard Hot 100 singles chart.

In 1993, Jackson performed the song at the Soul Train Awards in a chair, after suffering an injury in rehearsals.

In the UK and other parts of Europe, "Heal the World" was the biggest hit from the album; it sold 450,000 copies in the UK and spent five weeks at number two in 1992.

Jackson founded the "Heal the World Foundation" in 1992. The charity organization brought underprivileged children to Jackson's ranch to enjoy theme park rides that Jackson had built on the property. The foundation also sent millions of dollars around the globe to help children threatened by war and disease.

The Dangerous World Tour began on June 27, 1992, and finished on November 11, 1993. Jackson performed to 3.5 million people in 67 concerts. All profits from the concerts went to the "Heal the World Foundation", raising millions of dollars in relief.

Michael Jackson sold the broadcast rights to his Dangerous world tour to HBO for $20 million, a record-breaking deal that still stands.

Following the death of Ryan White, a teenager who became infected with HIV from a contaminated blood treatment, Michael helped draw public attention to HIV/AIDS, something that was still controversial at the time. Michael publicly pleaded with the Clinton Administration at Bill Clinton's Inaugural Gala to give more money to HIV/AIDS charities and research.

In a high-profile visit to Africa, Jackson visited several countries, among them Gabon and Egypt. His first stop to Gabon was greeted with a sizable reception of more than 100,000 people in "spiritual bedlam", some of them carrying signs that read, "Welcome Home Michael".

Michael Jackson

In his trip to the Ivory Coast, Jackson was crowned "King Sani" by a tribal chief. Michael Jackson then thanked the dignitaries in French and English, signed official documents formalizing his kingship and sat on a golden throne while presiding over ceremonial dances.

One of Jackson's most acclaimed performances came during the halftime show at Super Bowl XXVII. As the performances began, Jackson was catapulted onto the stage as fireworks went off behind him. As he landed on the canvass, he maintained a motionless "clenched fist, standing statue stance", dressed in a gold and black military outfit and sunglasses; he remained completely motionless while the crowd cheered. He then slowly removed his sunglasses, threw them away and began to sing and dance. His routine included four songs: "Jam", "Billie Jean", "Black or White" and "Heal the World". It was the first Super Bowl where the audience figures increased during the half-time show, and was viewed by 135 million Americans alone. As a result of the Super Bowl performance, Jackson's Dangerous album rose 90 places up the album chart.

Michael Jackson was given the "Living Legend Award" at the 35th Annual Grammy Awards in Los Angeles. "Black or White" was Grammy nominated for best vocal performance. "Jam" gained two nominations: Best R&B Vocal Performance and Best R&B Song.

On May 26 1994, Michael Jackson married singer-songwriter Lisa Marie Presley, the daughter of Elvis Presley. They divorced less than two years later.

1995–2000: HIStory and Blood on the Dance Floor

In 1995, Michael Jackson merged his Northern Songs catalog with Sony's publishing division creating Sony/ATV Music Publishing. Jackson retained half-ownership of the company, earned $95 million upfront as well as the rights to even more songs. Michael Jackson then released the double album HIStory: Past, Present and Future, Book I. The first disc, HIStory Begins, was a 15-track greatest hits album, and was later reissued as Greatest Hits – HIStory Vol. I in 2001, while the second disc, HIStory Continues, contained 15 new songs. HIStory Begins debuted at number one on the charts and has been certified for seven million shipments in the US, and it is the best-selling multiple-disc album of all-time, with 20 million copies (40 million units) sold worldwide and HIStory received a Grammy nomination for best album.

Michael Jackson

The first single released from the album was the double A-side "Scream/Childhood". "Scream" was a duet, performed with Michael Jackson's youngest sister Janet Jackson. The single had the highest debut on the Billboard Hot 100 at number five, and received a Grammy nomination for "Best Pop Collaboration with Vocals". "You Are Not Alone" was the second single released from HIStory and it holds the Guinness World Record for the first song ever to debut at number one on the Billboard Hot 100 chart. It was seen as a major artistic and commercial success, receiving a Grammy nomination for "Best Pop Vocal Performance".

In late 1995, Jackson was rushed to a hospital after collapsing during rehearsals for a televised performance. The incident was said to have been caused by stress related to a panic attack.

"Earth Song" was the third single released from HIStory, and topped the UK singles chart for six weeks over Christmas 1995; it sold a million copies, making it Jackson's most successful single in the UK.

The HIStory World Tour began on September 7, 1996, and finished on October 15, 1997. Jackson performed 82 concerts in 58 cities to over 4.5 million fans. The show, which visited five continents and 35 countries, became Jackson's most successful in terms of audience figures.

On November 14, 1996, during the Australian leg of the tour, Jackson married his dermatologist's nurse Deborah Rowe, with whom he fathered a son, Michael Joseph Jackson, Jr. (after their divorce his name was changed to Prince Michael Jackson), and a daughter, Paris Katherine Michael Jackson. Jackson and Rowe divorced in 1999.

In 1997, Jackson released an album of new material with remixes of hit singles from HIStory titled Blood on the Dance Floor: HIStory in the Mix. The album's five original songs were named "Blood On The Dance Floor", "Is It Scary?", "Ghosts", "Superfly Sister" and "Morphine". Of the new songs, three were released globally: the title track, "Ghosts", and "Is It Scary?". "Ghosts", "Superfly Sister" and "Morphine".

Michael Jackson

Of the new songs, three were released globally: the title track, "Ghosts", and "Is It Scary?". The title track reached number-one in the UK. The singles "Ghosts" and "Is It Scary" were based on a film created by Jackson called "Ghosts". The short film, written by Michael Jackson and Stephen King and directed by Stan Winston, features many special effects and dance moves choreographed to original music written by Michael Jackson. The music video for "Ghosts" is over 35 minutes long and is currently the World's Longest Music Video. Jackson dedicated the album to Elton John, who reportedly helped him through his addiction to painkillers, notably morphine.

Throughout June 1999, Michael Jackson was involved in a number of charitable events joining Luciano Pavarotti for a benefit concert in Modena, Italy. The concert was in support of War Child, and raised a million dollars for the refugees of Kosovo, as well as additional funds for the children of Guatemala. Later that month, Jackson organized a set of "Michael Jackson & Friends" benefit concerts in Germany and Korea. Other artists involved included Slash, The Scorpions, Boyz II Men, Luther Vandross, Mariah Carey, A. R. Rahman, Prabhu Deva Sundaram, Shobana Chandrakumar, Andrea Bocelli and Luciano Pavarotti. The proceeds went to the "Nelson Mandela Children's Fund", the Red Cross and UNESCO.

2000–2003: Invincible, Berlin and Martin Bashir

In 2000, Michael Jackson was listed in the book of Guinness World Records for his support of 39 charities, more than any other entertainer or personality. At the time, Michael Jackson was waiting for the licenses to the masters of his albums to revert to him; thus allowing him to promote his old material how he liked and preventing Sony from getting a cut of the profits. Jackson had expected this to occur early in the new millennium; however, due to various clauses in the contract, this revert date is still many years away. Michael Jackson began an investigation, and it emerged that the attorney who represented the singer in the deal was also representing Sony, creating a conflict of interest.

Jackson was also concerned about another conflict of interest as for a number of years, Sony had been pushing to buy all of Jackson's share in their music catalog venture. If Jackson's career or financial situation were to deteriorate, he would have to sell his entire music catalog. Thus, Sony had the most to gain from Jackson's career failing.

In October 2001, Invincible was released and debuted at number-one in thirteen countries. The singles released from the album include "You Rock My World", "Cry", and "Butterflies". Jackson and 35 other artists recorded a charity benefit single entitled "What More Can I Give" which was never released.

Just before the release of Invincible, Michael informed the head of Sony Music Entertainment, Tommy Mottola, that he was leaving Sony. As a result, all singles releases, video shootings and promotions concerning the Invincible album were cancelled.

On September 7 and September 10, 2001, Jackson organized a special 30th Anniversary celebration at Madison Square Garden for his 30th year of being a solo artist. Later, the show aired on November 13, 2001. It featured performances by Whitney Houston, Usher, Mýa, Billy Gilman, Britney Spears Shaggy, Rayvon, Rikrok, Destiny's Child, Monica, Missy Eilliot Deborah Cox, James Ingram, Gloria Estefan, Luther Vandross, Liza Minnelli, Lil' Romeo, Master P, 'N Sync, Spears the Jacksons Slash among other artist.

Invincible was a commercial success, debuting atop the charts in 13 countries and going on to sell approximately 10 million copies worldwide. It received double-platinum certification in the US. However, the sales for Invincible were notably low compared to his previous releases, due in part to a diminishing pop music industry, the lack of promotion, no supporting world tour, the label dispute, and of course, due to the ability to download just about any MP3 for free. The album spawned three singles, "You Rock My World", "Cry" and "Butterflies".

Michael's third child, Prince Michael Jackson II (also known as Blanket) was born in 2002

2003–2006:

In November 2003, Michael Jackson and Sony Records released a compilation of his number-one hits on CD and DVD titled Number Ones. The compilation has sold over six million copies worldwide. On the album's scheduled release date, while Michael Jackson was in Las Vegas filming the video for "One More Chance" (the only new song included in the Number Ones compilation). Jackson converted to the Nation of Islam on December 17, 2003. Later in 2005, because of his links with the Bahrain Royal Family, he converted to Sunni Islam.

Michael Jackson

Jackson relocated to the Gulf island of Bahrain, where he reportedly bought a house formerly owned by a Bahrain MP.

2006–present: Visionary, Tokyo and the World Music Awards

In 2006, Sony released the Visionary box set. He also visited the London office of the Guinness World Records. There, he received eight awards: "Most Successful Entertainer of All Time", "Youngest Vocalist to Top the US Singles Charts" (at the age of 11 as part of the Jackson Five), "First Vocalist to Enter the US Singles Chart at Number One" (for "You Are Not Alone"), "First Entertainer to Earn More Than 100 million Dollars in a Year", "Highest Paid Entertainer of All Time" ($125 in 1989), "First Entertainer to Sell More Than 100 Million Albums Outside the US", "Most Weeks at the Top of the US Albums Chart" (for the album Thriller) and "Most Successful Music Video" (for the music video Thriller).

On November 15, 2006, Michael Jackson received the Diamond Award, for selling over 100 million albums, at the World Music Awards.

On June 25, 2009, Michael collapsed at his rented mansion at 100 North Carolwood Drive in the Holmby Hills district of Los Angeles. Attempts at resuscitating him were unsuccessful. Michael was pronounced dead at 2:26 p.m.

"Music has been my outlet, my gift to all of the lovers in this world. Through it, my music, I know I will live forever." – Michael Jackson

THE MUSICIAN

THE MUSICIAN

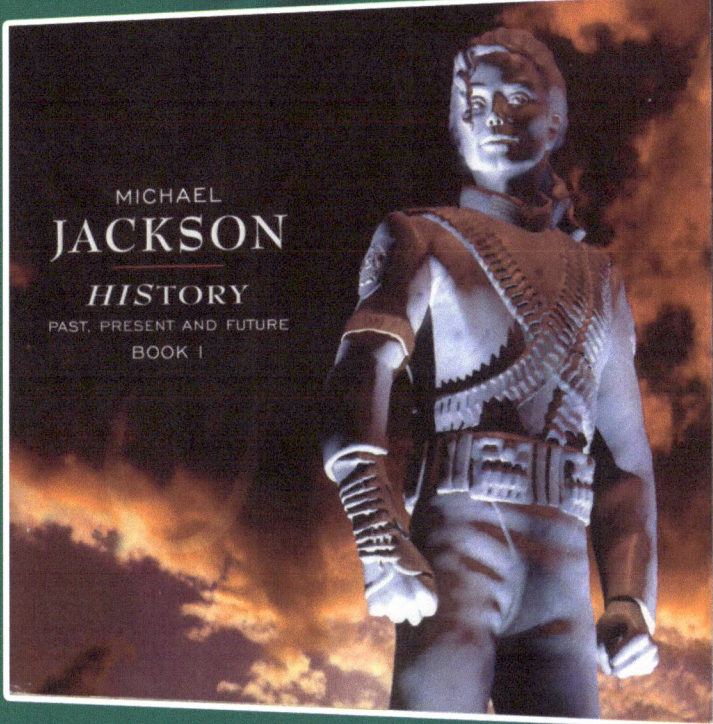

GOT TO BE THERE

Got To Be There (Got To Be There)
Got To Be There In The Morning
When She Says Hello To The World
Got To Be There (Got To Be There)
Got To Be There bring Her Good Times
And Show Her That She's My Girl
Ooo What A Feeling There'll Be
The Moment I Know She Loves Me
Cause When I look In Her Eyes I Realize
I Need Her Sharing The World Beside Me

So I Got To Be There (Got To Be There)
Got To Be There In The Morning And
Welcome Her Into My World
And show Her That She's My Girl
When She Says Hello World
(Got To Be There) (Got To Be There)

I Need Her Sharing The World Beside Me

That's Why I Got To Be There (Got To Be There)
Got To Be There Where Love Begin
And That's Everywhere She Goes
I Got To Be There So She Knows
That When She's With Me
She's Home (Home She's Home) (Home She's Home) Yea

(Got To Be There) Got To Be There, Got To Be There
(Got To Be There) Got To Be There, Got To Be There
(Got To Be There) Ooh Baby, Baby, Got To Be There
(Got To Be There) Got To Be There, Got To Be There

Michael's First Solo Single

OFF THE WALL

She's Out Of My Life

She's Out Of My Life
She's Out Of My Life
And I Don't Know Whether To Laugh Or Cry
I Don't Know Whether To Live Or Die
And It Cuts Like A Knife
She's Out Of My Life

It's Out Of My Hands
It's Out Of My Hands
To Think For Two Years She Was Here
And I Took Her For Granted I Was So Cavalier
Now The Way That It Stands
She's Out Of My Hands

So I've Learned That Love's Not Possession
And I've Learned That Love Won't Wait
Now I've Learned That Love Needs Expression
But I Learned Too Late

She's Out Of My Life
She's Out Of My Life
Damned Indecision And Cursed Pride
Kept My Love For Her Locked Deep Inside
And It Cuts Like A Knife
She's Out Of My Life

I Can't Help It

Looking In My Mirror
Took Me By Surprise
I Can't Help But See You
Running Often Through My Mind

Helpless Like A Baby
Sensual Disguise
I Can't Help But Love You
It's Getting Better All The Time

I Can't Help It If I Wanted To
I Wouldn't Help It Even If I Could
I Can't Help It If I Wanted To
I Wouldn't Help It, No

Love To Run My Fingers
Softly While You Sigh
Love Came And Possessed You
Bringing Sparkles To Your Eyes

Like A Trip To Heaven
Heaven Is The Prize
And I'm So Glad I Found You Girl
You're An Angel In Disguise

And I'm So Glad I Found You Girl
You're An Angel In Disguise

It's The Falling In Love

You're Not Like Anybody I Ever Knew
But That Don't Mean That
 I Don't Know Where We Are
And Though I Find Myself Attracted To You
This Time I'm Trying Not To Go Too Far, Cause

No Matter How It Starts It Ends The Same
Someone's Always Doing Someone More
Trading In The Passion For That Taste Of Pain
It's Only Gonna Happen Again

It's The Fallin' In Love That's Makin' Me High
It's The Being In Love That Makes Me Cry Cry Cry
It's The Fallin' In Love That's Makin' Me High
It's The Being In Love That Makes Me Cry Cry Cry
All Night... All Night

(Patti Austin)
And Though I'm Trying Not To Look In Your Eyes
Each Time I Do They Kind Of
 Burn Right Through Me
Don't Want To Lay Down In A Bed Full Of Lies
And Yet My Heart Is Saying Come And Do Me

Now We're Just A Web Of Mystery
A Possibility Of More To Come
I'd Rather Leave The Fantasy Of What Might Be
But Here I Go Falling Again

Get On The Floor

Ah Get On The Floor And Dance
Ah, On The Floor And Dance

So Get On The Floor
And Dance With Me
I Love The Way You Shake Your Thing
Especially

There's A Chance For Dancin'
All Night Long
There's A Chance For Groovin'
And It Will Be Soothing
With A Song

Then Why Don't You Just
Dance Across The Floor
'Cause There's A Chance For Chances
And The Chance Is Choosin'
And I Sure Would Like Just To Groove With You

No Need For Rejection
Determined To Be
Gonna Groove Gonna Move Ya
Gonna Say Things To Ya
Just Wait And See

Burn The Disco Out

There's A Steam Beat
And It's Comin' After You
You Can Take It
If You Only Let Your Feelings Through

So D.J. Spin The Sounds
There Ain't No Way That Your Gonna
Let Us Down
Gonna Dance Gonna Burn This Disco Out

Groove All Night
Keep The Boogie Alright
Get That Sound
Everybody Just Get On Down

Got A Hot Foot
Better Freak Across The Floor
Join The Party
And We'll Keep You Movin', That's For Sure

So D.J. Spin The Sounds
There Ain't No Way That Your Gonna
Sit Us Down
Gonna Dance 'Til We Burn This Disco Out

Groove All Night
Keep The Boogie Alright
Get That Sound
Everybody Just Get On Down

Once You Get The Beat Inside Your Feet
There Ain't No Way To Stop You Movin' Good
Now The Weekend's Come It's Time For Fun
You Got To Groove Just Like You Know You Should

People Now
Are You Ready
Won't You Rock Across The Room
Got A Feelin'
That We're Gonna Raise The Roof Off Soon

So D.J. Spin The Sounds
There Ain't No Way That Your Gonna
Sit Us Down
Gonna Dance 'Til We Burn This Disco Out

Groove All Night
Keep The Boogie Alright
Get That Sound
Everybody Just Get On Down

So D.J. Spin The Sounds
There Ain't No Way That Your Gonna
Sit Us Down
Gonna Dance 'Til We Burn This Disco Out

Groove All Night
Keep The Boogie Alright
Get That Sound
Everybody Just Get On Down

Gonna Dance, Gonna Shout
Gonna Burn This Disco Out
Gonna Dance, Gonna Shout
Gonna Burn This Disco Out
Gonna Dance, Gonna Shout
Gonna Burn This Disco Out

OFF THE WALL

Don't Stop 'Til You Get Enough

Lovely Is The Feelin' Now
Fever, Temperatures Risin' Now
Power (Ah Power) Is The Force The Vow
That Makes It Happen It Asks No Questions Why
So Get Closer (Closer Now)
To My Body Now Just Love Me
'Til You Don't Know How (Ooh)

Keep On With The Force Don't Stop
Don't Stop 'Til You Get Enough
Keep On With The Force Don't Stop
Don't Stop 'Til You Get Enough
Keep On With The Force Don't Stop
Don't Stop 'Til You Get Enough
Keep On With The Force Don't Stop
Don't Stop 'Til You Get Enough

Touch Me And I Feel On Fire
Ain't Nothin' Like A Love Desire (Ooh)
I'm Melting (I'm Melting)
Like Hot Candle Wax Sensation (Ah Sensation)
Lovely Where We're At (Ooh)
So Let Love Take Us Through The Hours
I Won't Be Complainin'
'Cause This Is Love Power (Ooh)

Heartbreak Enemy Despise
Eternal (Ah Eternal)
Love Shines In My Eyes (Ooh)
So Let Love Take Us Through The Hours
I Won't Be Complainin' (No No)
'Cause Your Love Is Alright, Alright

Lovely Is The Feeling Now I Won't Be Complainin'
The Force Is Love Power

I Wanna Rock With You

Girl, close your eyes
Let that rhythm get into you
Dont try to fight it
There aint nothin that you can do
Relax your mind
Lay back and groove with mine
You got to feel the heat
And we can ride the boogie
Share that beat of love

I wanna rock with you (all night)
Dance you into day (sunlight)
I wanna rock with you (all night)
Were gonna rock the night away

Out on the floor
There aint nobody there but us
Girl, when you dance
Theres a magic that must be love
Just take it slow
cause we got so far to go
When you feel that heat
And were gonna ride the boogie
Share that beat of love

And when the groove is dead and gone (yeah)
You know that love survives
So we can rock forever, on

I wanna rock with you
I wanna groove with you
I wanna rock with you

Working Day And Night

Ooh My Honey
You Got Me Workin' Day And Night
Ooh My Sugar
You Got Me Workin' Day And Night

Scratch My Shoulder
It's Aching, Make It Feel Alright
When This Is Over
Lovin' You Will Be So Right

I Often Wonder If Lovin' You
Will Be Tonight
But What Is Love Girl
If I'm Always Out Of Sight (Ooh)

You Got Me Workin' Day And Night
And I'll Be Workin'
From Sun Up To Midnight

You Got Me Workin' Workin' Day And Night
You Got Me Workin' Workin' Day And Night
You Got Me Workin' Workin' Day And Night
You Got Me Workin' Workin' Day And Night

You Say That Workin'
Is What A Man's Supposed To Do
But I Say It Ain't Right
If I Can't Give Sweet Love To You (Ah)

I'm Tired Of Thinkin'
Of What My Life's Supposed To Be (Well)
Soon Enough Darlin'
This Love Will Be Reality (Ah Ah)

How Can You Live Girl
'Cause Love For Us Was Meant To Be (Well)
Then You Must Be Seein'
Some Other Guy Instead Of Me (Ooh)

You Say That Workin'
Is What A Man's Supposed To Do
But I Say It Ain't Right
If I Can't Give Sweet Love To You (Well, Ah)

How Can You Live Girl
'Cause Love For Us Was Meant To Be (Well)
Then You Must Be Seein' (Woo)
Some Other Guy Instead Of Me (Ooh)

Get On The Floor

Ah Get On The Floor And Dance
Ah, On The Floor And Dance

So Get On The Floor
And Dance With Me
I Love The Way You Shake Your Thing
Especially

There's A Chance For Dancin'
All Night Long
There's A Chance For Groovin'
And It Will Be Soothing
With A Song

Then Why Don't You Just
Dance Across The Floor
'Cause There's A Chance For Chances
And The Chance Is Choosin'
And I Sure Would Like Just To Groove With You

Off The Wall

When The World Is On Your Shoulder
Gotta Straighten Up Your Act And Boogie Down
If You Can't Hang With The Feeling
Then There Ain't No Room
For You This Part Of Town
'Cause We're The Party People Night And Day
Livin' Crazy That's The Only Way

So Tonight Gotta Leave That
Nine To Five Upon The Shelf
And Just Enjoy Yourself
Groove, Let The Madness In The Music Get To You
Life Ain't So Bad At All
If You Live It Off The Wall
Life Ain't So Bad At All (Live Life Off The Wall)
Live Your Life Off The Wall (Live It Off The Wall)

You Can Shout Out All You Want To
'Cause There Ain't No Sin In Folks All Getting Loud
If You Take The Chance And Do It
Then There Ain't No One Who's Gonna Put You Down
'Cause We're The Party People Night And Day
Livin' Crazy That's The Only Way

Do What You Want To Do
There Ain't No Rules It's Up To You
(Ain't No Rules It's All Up To You)
It's Time To Come Alive
And Party On Right Through The Night (All Right)

Gotta Hide Your Inhibitions
Gotta Let That Fool Loose Deep Inside Your Soul
Want To See An Exhibition
Better Do It Now Before You Get To Old
'Cause We're The Party People Night And Day
Livin' Crazy That's The Only Way

Girlfriend

Girlfriend
I'm Gonna Tell Your Boyfriend (Yeah)
Tell Him (Woo Hoo)
Exactly What We're Doin' (Yeah)
Tell Him What You Do To Me
Late At Night When The Wind Is Free

Girlfriend
I'm Gonna Show Your Boyfriend (Yeah)
Show Him (Woo Hoo)
The Letters I've Been Savin' (Yeah)
Show Him How You Feel Inside
An' How Love Could Not Be Denied (Oh No)

We're Gonna Have To Tell Him
You'll Only Be A Girlfriend Of Mine
Do-Doot-Do, [Etc.]

We're Gonna Have To Tell Him
You'll Only Be A Girlfriend Of Mine

Girlfriend You Better Tell Your Boyfriend (Yeah)
Tell Him (Woo Hoo)
Exactly What We're Doin' (Yeah)
Tell Him What He Needs To Know
Or He May Never Let You Go

THRILLER

Wanna Be Startin' Somethin'

I Said You Wanna Be Startin' Somethin'
You Got To Be Startin' Somethin'
I Said You Wanna Be Startin' Somethin'
You Got To Be Startin' Somethin'
It's Too High To Get Over (Yeah, Yeah)
Too Low To Get Under (Yeah, Yeah)
You're Stuck In The Middle (Yeah, Yeah)
And The Pain Is Thunder (Yeah, Yeah)
It's Too High To Get Over (Yeah, Yeah)
Too Low To Get Under (Yeah, Yeah)
You're Stuck In The Middle (Yeah, Yeah)
And The Pain Is Thunder (Yeah, Yeah)

I Took My Baby To The Doctor
With A Fever, But Nothing He Found
By The Time This Hit The Street
They Said She Had A Breakdown
Someone's Always Tryin' Start My
Baby Cryin' Talkin', Squealin', Lyin'
Sayin' You Just Wanna Be Startin' Somethin'

(repeat)

You Love To Pretend That You're Good
When You're Always Up To No Good
You Really Can't Make Him Hate Her
So Your Tongue Became A Razor
Someone's Always Tryin' To Keep My Baby
Cryin' Treacherous, Cunnin', Declinin'
You Got My Baby Cryin'

(repeat)

You're A Vegetable, You're A Vegetable
Still they hate you, You're A Vegetable
You're Just A Buffet, You're A Vegetable
They Eat Off Of You, You're A Vegetable

Billie Jean Is Always Talkin'
When Nobody Else Is Talkin'
Tellin' Lies And Rubbin' Shoulders
So They Called Her Mouth A Motor
Someone's Always Tryin' To Start My Baby
Cryin' Talkin', Squealin', Spyin'
Sayin' You Just Wanna Be Startin' Somethin'

(repeat)

If You Cant Feed Your Baby (Yeah, Yeah)
Then Don't Have A Baby (Yeah, Yeah)
And Don't Think Maybe (Yeah, Yeah)
If You Can't Feed Your Baby (Yeah, Yeah)
You'll Be Always Tryin'
To Stop That Child From Cryin'
Hustlin', Stealin', Lyin'
Now Baby's Slowly Dyin'

Lift Your Head Up High
And Scream Out To The World
I Know I Am Someone
And Let The Truth Unfurl
No One Can Hurt You Now
Because You Know What's True
Yes, I Believe In Me
So You Believe In You
Help Me Sing It, Ma Ma Se,
Ma Ma Sa, Ma Ma Coo Sa
Ma Ma Se, Ma Ma Sa,
Ma Ma Coo Sa

And Let The Truth Unfurl
No One Can Hurt You Now
Because You Know What's True
Yes, I Believe In Me
So You Believe In You
Help Me Sing It, Ma Ma Se,
Ma Ma Sa, Ma Ma Coo Sa
Ma Ma Se, Ma Ma Sa,
Ma Ma Coo Sa

Baby Be Mine

I Don't Need No Dreams
When I'm By Your Side
Every Moment Takes Me To Paradise
Darlin', Let Me Hold You
Warm You In My Arms And Melt Your
Fears Away
Show You All The Magic
That A Perfect Love Can Make
I Need You Night And Day
So Baby, Be Mine
(Baby You Gotta BeMine)
And Girl I'll Give You All I Got
To Give So Baby, Be My Girl
And We Can Share This Ecstasy
As Long As We Believe In Love

I Won't Give You Reason
To Change Your Mind
(I Guess It's Still You Thrill Me, Baby,
Be Mine)
You Are All The Future That I Desire
Girl, I Need To Hold You Share My
Feelings In The Heat Of Love's Embrace
Show You All The Passion Burning In My
Heart Today It's Never Gonna Fade
So Baby, Be Mine (Baby You Gotta Be Mine)
And Girl I'll Give You All I Got To Give
So Baby, Be My Girl (All The Time)
You're Everything This World Could Be
The Reason That I Live

Won't You Stay With Me
Until The Mornin' Sun
I Promise You Now That The Dawn Will
Be Different
Lady Can't You See That Heaven's
Just Begun
It's Livin' Here Inside Our Hearts

There'll Be No More Mountains
For Us To Climb (I Can't Be Still You
Thrill Me, Baby, Be Mine)
This Will Be A Love Lasting For All Time
Girl You Got To Hold Me
We Can Touch The Sky And
Light The Darkest Day
Hold Me, Only You And I Can Make
Sweet Love This Way
There's No More I Can Say
So Baby, Be Mine (Baby You Gotta Be Mine)
And Girl I'll Give You All I Got To Give
So Baby, Be My (All The Time)
You're Everything This World Could Be
The Reason That I Live
Baby Be My Girl
And Girl I'll Give You All I Got To Give
So Baby, Be Mine, Baby, Be Mine
You're Everything This World Could Be To Me

C'mon, Girl, C'mon Girl
So Baby, Be Mine
You're Everything This World Could Be To Me
C'mon, Girl, C'mon Girl

The Girl Is Mine

(Michael) Every Night She Walks Right In
My Dreams Since I Met Her From The Start
I'm So Proud I Am The Only One Who Is
Special In Her Heart The Girl Is Mine The
Doggone Girl Is Mine I Know She's Mine
Because The Doggone Girl Is Mine

(Paul) I Don't Understand The Way You Think
Saying That She's Yours Not Mine Sending
Roses And Your Silly Dreams Really Just A
Waste Of Time Because She's Mine The
Doggone Girl Is Mine Don't Waste Your Time
Because The Doggone Girl Is Mine

(Paul) I Love You More Than He
(Take You Anywhere)

(Michael) Well I Love You Endlessly
(Loving We Will Share)

(Michael & Paul) So Come And
Go With Me Two On The Town

(Michael) But We Both Cannot Have Her
So It's One Or The Other
And One Day You'll Discover
That She's My Girl Forever And Ever

(Paul) I Don't Build Your Hopes
To Be Let Down 'Cause I Really Feel It's Time

(Michael) I Know She'll Tell You I'm The One
For Her 'Cause She Said I Blow Her Mind
The Girl Is Mine The Doggone Girl Is Mine
Don't Waste Your Time Because The Doggone
Girl Is Mine

(Michael & Paul) She's Mine, She's Mine
No, No, No, She's Mine The Girl Is Mine, The
Girl Is Mine The Girl Is Mine, The Girl Is Mine

(Paul)The Girl Is Mine, (Yep) She's Mine
The Girl Is Mine, (Yep) She's Mine

(Michael) Don't Waste Your Time
Because The Doggone Girl Is Mine
The Girl Is Mine, The Girl Is Mine

(Paul) Michael, We're Not Going To Fight
About This, Okay

(Michael) Paul, I Think I Told You,
I'm A Lover Not A Fighter

(Paul) I've Heard It All Before, Michael
She Told Me That I'm Her Forever Lover,
You Know, Don't You Remember

(Michael) Well, After Loving Me,
She Said She Couldn't Love Another

(Paul) Is That What She Said

(Michael) Yes, She Said It, You Keep Dreaming

(Paul) I Don't Believe It

(Michael & Paul)The Girl Is Mine
(Mine, Mine, Mine)

THRILLER

It's Close To Midnight And Something Evil's
Lurking In The Dark Under The Moonlight
You See A Sight That Almost Stops Your Heart
You Try To Scream But Terror Takes The Sound
Before You Make It You Start To Freeze As
Horror Looks You Right Between The Eyes,
You're Paralyzed
'Cause This Is Thriller, Thriller Night
And No One's Gonna Save You From The
Beast About Strike You Know It's Thriller,
Thriller Night You're Fighting For Your Life
Inside A Killer, Thriller Tonight

You Hear The Door Slam And Realize There's
Nowhere Left To Run You Feel The Cold Hand
And Wonder If You'll Ever See The Sun
You Close Your Eyes And Hope That This Is
Just Imagination, Girl But All The While You
Hear A Creature Creepin' Up Behind
You're Out Of Time

'Cause This Is Thriller, Thriller Night
There Ain't No Second Chance Against
The Thing With Forty Eyes Girl
You Know It's Thriller, Thriller Night
You're Fighting For Your Life Inside Of
Killer, Thriller Tonight
Night Creatures Call
And The Dead Start To Walk In Their Masquerade
There's No Escapin' The Jaws Of The Alien This Time
(They're Open Wide)
This Is The End Of Your Life
They're Out To Get You, There's Demons Closing
In On Every Side They Will Possess You Unless You
Change The Number On Your Dial
Now Is The Time For You And I To Cuddle Close Together
All Thru The Night I'll Save You From The Terror
On The Screen, I'll Make You See

That This Is Thriller, Thriller Night
'Cause I Can Thrill You More Than Any Ghost
Would Dare To Try (Thriller, Thriller Night)
So Let Me Hold You Tight And Share A Killer,
Diller, Chiller Thriller Here Tonight
Cause This Is Thriller, Thriller Night
Girl I Can Thrill You More Than Any Ghost
Would Dare To Try (Thriller, Thriller Night)
So Let Me Hold You Tight And Share A
Thriller, Chiller

(I'm Gonna Thrill Tonight)

(Vincent Price) Darkness Falls Across The Land
The Midnite Hour Is Close At Hand
Creatures Crawl In Search Of Blood
To Terrorize Y'awl's Neighbourhood
And Whosoever Shall Be Found
Without The Soul For Getting Down
Must Stand And Face The Hounds Of Hell
And Rot Inside A Corpse's Shell
The Foulest Stench Is In The Air
The Funk Of Forty Thousand Years
And Grizzy Ghouls From Every Tomb
Are Closing In To Seal Your Doom
And Though You Fight To Stay Alive
Your Body Starts To Shiver
For No Mere Mortal Can Resist
The Evil Of The Thriller

THRILLER

Beat It

They Told Him Don't You Ever Come
Around Here
Don't Wanna See Your Face, You Better Disappear
The Fire's In Their Eyes And
Their Words Are Really Clear
So Beat It, Just Beat It

You Better Run, You Better Do What You Can
Don't Wanna See No Blood,
Don't Be A Macho Man
You Wanna Be Tough, Better Do What You Can
So Beat It, But You Wanna Be Bad

Just Beat It, Beat It, Beat It, Beat It
No One Wants To Be Defeated
Showin' How Funky Strong Is Your Fight
It Doesn't Matter Who's Wrong Or Right
Just Beat It, Beat It
Just Beat It, Beat It
Just Beat It, Beat It
Just Beat It, Beat It

They're Out To Get You, Better Leave
While You Can
Don't Wanna Be A Boy, You Wanna Be A Man
You Wanna Stay Alive, Better Do What You Can
So Beat It, Just Beat It

You Have To Show Them That You're
Really Not Scared
You're Playin' With Your Life,
This Ain't No Truth Or Dare
They'll Kick You, Then They Beat You,
Then They'll Tell You It's Fair
So Beat It, But You Wanna Be Bad

Just Beat It, Beat It, Beat It, Beat It
No One Wants To Be Defeated
Showin' How Funky Strong Is Your Fight
It Doesn't Matter Who's Wrong Or Right

Just Beat It, Beat It, Beat It, Beat It
No One Wants To Be Defeated
Showin' How Funky Strong Is Your Fight
It Doesn't Matter Who's Wrong Or Right
Just Beat It, Beat It, Beat It, Beat It

Beat It, Beat It, Beat It, Beat It
No One Wants To Be Defeated
Showin' How Funky Strong Is Your Fight
It Doesn't Matter Who's Wrong Or Right

Just Beat It, Beat It, Beat It, Beat It
No One Wants To Be Defeated
Showin' How Funky Strong Is Your Fight
It Doesn't Matter Who's Wrong
Or Who's Right

Just Beat It, Beat It, Beat It, Beat It
No One Wants To Be Defeated
Showin' How Funky Strong Is Your Fight
It Doesn't Matter Who's Wrong Or Right
Just Beat It, Beat It
Beat It, Beat It, Beat It

Billie Jean

She Was More Like A Beauty Queen
From A Movie Scene
I Said Don't Mind, But What Do You
Mean I Am The One
Who Will Dance On The Floor In The Round
She Said I Am The One Who Will Dance
On The Floor In The Round

She Told Me Her Name Was Billie Jean,
As She Caused A Scene
Then Every Head Turned With Eyes
That Dreamed Of Being The One
Who Will Dance On The Floor In The Round

People Always Told Me Be Careful
Of What You Do Don't Go Around
Breaking Young Girls' Hearts
And Mother Always Told Me Be
Careful Of Who You Love
And Be Careful Of What You Do
'Cause The Lie Becomes The Truth

Billie Jean Is Not My Lover
She's Just A Girl Who Claims That
I Am The One
But The Kid Is Not My Son
She Says I Am The One, But The
Kid Is Not My Son

For Forty Days And Forty Nights
The Law Was On Her Side
But Who Can Stand When She's In Demand
Her Schemes And Plans
'Cause We Danced On The Floor In The Round
So Take My Strong Advice, Just Remember
To Always Think Twice

She Told My Baby We'd Danced 'Till Three
Then She Looked At Me
Then Showed A Photo My Baby Cried
His Eyes Looked Like Mine
Go On Dance On The Floor In The Round, Baby

People Always Told Me Be Careful Of What You Do
Don't Go Around Breaking Young Girls' Hearts
She Came And Stood Right By Me
Then The Smell Of Sweet Perfume
This Happened Much Too Soon
She Called Me To Her Room

Billie Jean Is Not My Lover
She's Just A Girl Who Claims That I Am The One
But The Kid Is Not My Son
Billie Jean Is Not My Lover
She's Just A Girl Who Claims That I Am The One
But The Kid Is Not My Son
She Says I Am The One, But The Kid Is Not My Son
She Says I Am The One, She Says He Is My Son
She Says I Am The One
Billie Jean Is Not My Lover
Billie Jean Is Not My Lover
Billie Jean Is Not My Lover
Billie Jean Is Not My Lover
Billie Jean Is Not My Lover
Billie Jean Is Not My Lover

Human Nature

Looking Out
Across The Night-Time
The City Winks A Sleepless Eye
Hear Her Voice
Shake My Window
Sweet Seducing Sighs

Get Me Out
Into The Night-Time
Four Walls Won't Hold Me Tonight
If This Town
Is Just An Apple
Then Let Me Take A Bite

If They Say
Why, Why, Tell 'Em That Is Human Nature
Why, Why, Does He Do Me That Way
If They Say
Why, Why, Tell 'Em That Is Human Nature
Why, Why, Does He Do Me That Way

Reaching Out
Touch A Stranger
Electric Eyes Are Ev'rywhere
See That Girl
She Knows I'm Watching
She Likes The Way I Stare

If They Say
Why, Why, Tell 'Em That Is Human Nature
Why, Why, Does He Do Me That Way
If They Say
Why, Why, Tell 'Em That Is Human Nature
Why, Why, Does He Do Me That Way
I Like Livin' This Way
I Like Lovin' This Way

Looking Out
Across The Morning
The City's Heart Begins To Beat
Reaching Out
I Touch Her Shoulder
I'm Dreaming Of The Street

If They Say
Why, Why, Tell 'Em That Is Human Nature
Why, Why, Does He Do Me That Way
If They Say
Why, Why, Ooh Tell 'Em
Why, Why, Does He Do Me That Way
If They Say Why, Why, Cha, Cha, Cha
Why, Why, Does He Do Me That Way
If They Say
Why, Why, Why Ooh Tell 'Em
Why, Why, Does He Do Me That Way
If They Say Why, Why, Ooh Tell 'Em

Why, Why, Does He Do Me That Way
If They Say Why, Why, Da ,Da, Da
Why, Why, Does He Do Me That Way
I Like Livin' This Way

THRILLER

P.Y.T. (Pretty Young Thing)

Where Did You Come From Lady
And Ooh Won't You Take Me There
Right Away Won't You Baby
Tendoroni You've Got To Be
Spark My Nature
Sugar Fly With Me
Don't You Know Now
Is The Perfect Time
We Can Make It Right
Hit The City Lights
Then Tonight Ease The Lovin' Pain
Let Me Take You To The Max

I Want To Love You (P.Y.T.)
Pretty Young Thing
You Need Some Lovin' (T.L.C.)
Tender Lovin' Care
And I'll Take You There
I Want To Love You (P.Y.T.)
Pretty Young Thing
You Need Some Lovin' (T.L.C.)
Tender Lovin' Care
I'll Take You There

Nothin' Can Stop This Burnin'
Desire To Be With You
Gotta Get To You Baby
Won't You Come, It's Emergency
Cool My Fire Yearnin'
Honey, Come Set Me Free
Don't You Know Now Is The Perfect Time
We Can Dim The Lights
Just To Make It Right
In The Night
Hit The Lovin' Spot
I'll Give You All That I've Got

I Want To Love You (P.Y.T.)
Pretty Young Thing
You Need Some Lovin' (T.L.C.)
Tender Lovin' Care
And I'll Take You There
Yes, I Will, Yes I Will
I Want To Love You (P.Y.T.)
Pretty Young Thing
You Need Some Lovin' (T.L.C.)
Tender Lovin' Care
I'll Take You There Yes, I Will

Pretty Young Things, Repeat After Me
[Michael] I Say Na Na Na
[P.Y.T.'S] Na Na Na
[Michael] Na Na Na Na
[P.Y.T.'S] Na Na Na Na Na
[Michael] Na Na Na Na
[P.Y.T.'S] Na Na Na
[Michael] I Say Na Na Na Na Na
[P.Y.T.'S] Na Na Na Na Na
[Michael] I'll Take You There

I Want To Love You (P.Y.T.)
Pretty Young Thing
You Need Some Lovin' (T.L.C.)
Tender Lovin' Care
And I'll Take You There
I Want To Love You (P.Y.T.)
Pretty Young Thing
You Need Some Lovin' (T.L.C.)
Tender Lovin' Care
I'll Take You There

Lady In My Life

There'll Be No Darkness Tonight
Lady Our Love Will Shine
Just Put Your Trust In My Heart
And Meet Me In Paradise, Girl
You're Every Wonder In This World To Me
A Treasure Time Won't Steal Away

So Listen To My Heart
Lay Your Body Close To Mine
Let Me Fill You With My Dreams
I Can Make You Feel Alright
And Baby Through The Years
Gonna Love You More Each Day
So I Promise You Tonight
That You'll Always Be The Lady In My Life

Lay Back In My Tenderness
Let's Make This A Night We Won't Forget
Girl, I Need Your Sweet Caress
Reach Out To A Fantasy
Two Hearts In The Beat Of Ecstasy
Come To Me, Girl

And I Will Keep You Warm
Through The Shadows Of The Night
Let Me Touch You With My Love
I Can Make You Feel So Right
And Baby Through The Years
Even When We're Old And Gray
I Will Love You More Each Day
'Cause You Will Always Be The Lady In My Life

Stay With Me
I Want You To Stay With Me...

Carousel

She's From A World
Of Popcorn And Candy
Pony Rides For A Dime
Little Children Laughing

I'm From A World
Of Disappointments And Confusions
But I Want Her To Be Mine
I Started Talking
She Kept On Walking
She Disappeared Into The Crowd

I Lost My Heart
On The Carousel
To A Circus Girl
Who Left My Heart In Pieces
Lost My Heart
On The Carousel
To A Circus Girl
Who Ran Away

Two Different People
In Love For An Instant
To See That The Circus Came Today
Sometimes I Can Hear The Calliope
And I Can Hear Her Calling Me.

I Lost My Heart
On The Carousel
To A Circus Girl
Who Left My Heart In Pieces
Lost My Heart
On The Carousel
To A Circus Girl
Who Ran Away

I Lost My Heart
On The Carousel
To A Circus Girl

BAD

BAD

Your Butt Is Mine Gonna Take You Right
Just Show Your Face In Broad Daylight
I'm Telling You On How I Feel
Gonna Hurt Your Mind Don't Shoot To
Kill Come On, Come On,
Lay It On Me All Right...

I'm Giving You On Count Of Three
To Show Your Stuff Or Let It Be . . .
I'm Telling You Just Watch Your Mouth
I Know Your Game What You're About

Well They Say The Sky's The Limit
And To Me That's Really True
But My Friend You Have Seen Nothing
Just Wait 'Til I Get Through
Because I'm Bad, I'm Bad
Come On You Know I'm Bad, I'm Bad
You Know It You Know I'm Bad, I'm Bad
Come On, You Know And The Whole
World Has To Answer Right Now
Just To Tell You Once Again, Who's Bad

The Word Is Out You're Doin' Wrong
Gonna Lock You Up Before Too Long,
Your Lyin' Eyes Gonna Take You Right
So Listen Up Don't Make A Fight,
Your Talk Is Cheap You're Not A Man
You're Throwin' Stones To Hide Your Hands

Well They Say The Sky's
The Limit
And To Me That's Really True
But My Friend You Have
Seen Nothing
Just Wait 'Til I Get Through
Because I'm Bad, I'm Bad
Come On You Know I'm Bad, I'm Bad
You Know It You Know I'm Bad, I'm Bad
Come On, You Know
And The Whole World Has To
Answer Right Now
Just To Tell You Once Again,
Who's Bad

If We Change The World Tomorrow
This Could Be A Better Place
If You Don't Like What I'm Sayin'
Then Won't You Slap My Face

Because I'm Bad, I'm Bad Come On
You Know I'm Bad, I'm Bad
You Know It You Know I'm Bad,
I'm Bad You Know It You Know
Woo! Woo! Woo!

You Know I'm Bad, I'm Bad Come
On You Know I'm Bad, I'm Bad You
Know It You Know It You Know,
You Know You Know Come on And
The Whole World Has To Answer
Right Now Just To Tell You Once
Again

You Know I'm Hoo! I'm Bad You
Know It You Know I'm Bad I'm Bad Baby
You Know You Know You Know You Know It
Come On And The Whole World Has To
Answer Right Now Just To Tell You
Once Again . . .

The Way You Make Me Feel

Hey Pretty Baby With The
High Heels On
You Give Me Fever
Like I've Never, Ever Known
You're Just A Product Of Loveliness
I Like The Groove Of Your Walk,
Your Talk, Your Dress
I Feel Your Fever
From Miles Around
I'll Pick You Up In My Car
And We'll Paint The Town
Just Kiss Me Baby
And Tell Me Twice
That You're The One For Me

The Way You Make Me Feel
You Really Turn Me On
You Knock Me Off Of My Feet
My Lonely Days Are Gone

I Like The Feelin' You're Givin' Me
Just Hold Me Baby And I'm In Ecstasy
Oh I'll Be Workin' From Nine To Five
To Buy You Things To Keep
You By My Side
I Never Felt So In Love Before
Just Promise Baby, You'll
Love Me Forevermore
I Swear I'm Keepin' You Satisfied
'Cause You're The One For Me
The Way You Make Me Feel
You Really Turn Me On
You Knock Me Off Of My Feet
Now Baby Hee!
My Lonely Days Are Gone

Go On Girl! Go On! Hee! Hee! Aaow!
Go On Girl!

I Never Felt So In Love Before
Promise Baby, You'll Love Me Forevermore
I Swear I'm Keepin' You Satisfied
'Cause You're The One For Me
The Way You Make Me Feel
You Really Turn Me On
You Knock Me Off Of My Feet
Now Baby Hee!
My Lonely Days Are Gone
The Way You Make Me Feel
You Really Turn Me On
You Knock Me Off Of My Feet
Now Baby Hee!
My Lonely Days Are Gone
Ain't Nobody's Business
Ain't Nobody's Business
Ain't Nobody's Business
Ain't Nobody's Business
But Mine And My Baby's
Hee Hee! Aaow!

Give It To Me-Give Me Some Time
Come On Be My Girl-I Wanna
Be With Mine Ain't Nobody's
Business Ain't Nobody's Business
But Mine And My Baby's
Go On Girl! Aaow!
My Lonely Days Are Gone

Hee Hee! Aaow!
Chika-Chika
Chika-Chika-Chika

Speed Demon

I'm Headed For The Border
It's On My Mind
And Nothin' Really Matters
I've Got To Be On Time
Look In The View Mirror
Is He Hot On My Tracks
Is He Getting Nearer
I Feel Some Heat Is On
My Back

Speedin' On The Freeway
Gotta Get A Leadway
Doin' It On The Highway
Gotta Have It My Way
Mind Is Like A Compass
I'm Stoppin' At Nothin'
Pull Over Boy And
Get Your Ticket Right . . .

And Nothin' Gonna Stop Me
Ain't No Stop And Go
I'm Speedin' On The Midway
I Gotta Really Burn This Road

Speedin' On The Freeway
Gotta Get The Leadway
Doin' It On The Highway
Gotta Have It My Way
Mind Is Like A Compass
I'm Stoppin' At Nothin'
Pull Over Boy And
Get Your Ticket Right . . .

Speed Demon, You're The
Very Same One Who Said The
Future's In Your Hands The Life
You Save Could Be Your Own
You're Preachin' 'Bout My
Life Like You're The Law
Gonna Live Each Day And Hour
Like For Me There's No Tomorrow

Go! Go! Go! Aaow!

Speedin' On The Freeway
Gotta Get The Leadway
Got Fire In My Pocket
I Just Lit A Rocket

Pull Over Boy And
Get Your Ticket Right
Pull Over Boy And
Get Your Ticket
Pull Over Boy And
Eat Your Ticket
Pull Over Boy
Pull Over Boy And
Get Your Ticket Right

Get Your Ticket Right

Pull Over Boy Get Your Ticket
Right Pull Over Boy
And Get Your Ticket Right
Pull Over Boy Pull Over Boy
Get Your Ticket Eat Your Ticket
Get Your Ticket Eat Yo', Get Yo'
Hoo! Aaow! Get Your Ticket Right.

BAD

Liberian Girl

Liberian Girl . . .
You Came And You Changed
My World
A Love So Brand New
Liberian Girl . . .
You Came And You Changed
Me Girl
A Feeling So True

Liberian Girl
You Know That You Came
And You Changed My World,
Just Like In The Movies,
With Two Lovers In A Scene
And She Says . . .
"Do You Love Me"
And He Says So Endlessly . . .
"I Love You, Liberian Girl"

Liberian Girl . . .
More Precious Than
Any Pearl
Your Love So Complete
Liberian Girl . . .
You Kiss Me Then,
Ooh, The World
You Do This To Me

Liberian Girl
You Know That You Came
And You Changed My World,
Just Like In The Movies,
With Two Lovers In A Scene
And She Says,

"Do You Love Me"
And He Says So Endlessly
"I Love You, Liberian Girl"
(Naku Penda Piya-Naku Taka
Piya-Mpenziwe)
(I Love You Too-I Want You
Too-My Love)

(Girl) I Love You Liberian Girl,
All The Time
(Girl) I Love You Liberian Girl,
All The Time
(Girl) I Love You Liberian Girl,
All The Time
(Girl) I Love You
I Love You Baby
(Girl) I Want You
I Love You Baby
(Girl) Ooh! I Love You Baby, I Want
You Baby, Ooh!

Just Good Friends

[Michael] I Watched You On The Floor
Cheek To Cheek
She's Getting To You
You Didn't See-Her Eyes On Me-No
She Looked Right Through You
(Before You Make) (A Big Mistake)
Remember That Looks Can Fool You
Babe, Hee!

There's Something I Would
Sure Appreciate
(If You Can Keep A Secret)

Baby Loves Me But She Never Shows
She Cares
(No, You Won't See Her Kiss
And Hug Me)
Baby Loves Me No She Acts Like I'm
Not There (That Doesn't Mean She
Doesn't Love Me-Ooo)

If They Ask Her
Tell 'Em That We're Just
Good Friends . . .
Just Good Friends . . .

[Stevie] You Better Take Advice
Never Trust-First Impressions
I Tried To Hide This Affair
From Their Suspicions

So Even If She's Asking You To Stay
You Better Know Where You Stand

Now If They Ask You
Jus' Tell 'Em That We're Just
Good Friends . . .

Yes . . . Just Good Friends
Just Good Friends . . .

[Michael] Listen Up, Hee . . . We've Got A
Problem Here
[Stevie] I Can See The Signs
[Michael] I Guess The Lady
[Both] Is Still Making Up Her Mind
(Say We're Just Good Friends)

[Stevie] Baby Loves Me
Though She Never Shows She Cares
No You Won't See Her Kiss
And Hug Me (Just Good Friends)
(My Baby Loves Me)

[Michael] Though She Acts Like I'm Not
There You Doggone Lover, Hee . . .
[Stevie] Aaow! (Doot-Do-Do-Doo . . .)

Don't You Wanna Know? My
Baby Loves Me
Though She Never Shows She Cares
(Never Shows She Cares)

[Michael] Hee! Hee!
[Stevie] She Doesn't Kiss And Hug Me
(Just Good Friends)

[Michael] My Baby Loves Me
She Love Me, She Love Me,
Hee! Hee! Hee! Hoo! Hoo!

Another Part Of Me

We're Takin' Over
We Have The Truth
This Is The Mission
To See It Through

Don't Point Your Finger
Not Dangerous
This Is Our Planet
You're One Of Us

We're Sendin' Out
A Major Love
And This Is Our
Message To You
(Message To You)
The Planets Are Linin' Up
We're Bringin' Brighter Days
They're All In Line
Waitin' For You
Can't You See . . . ?
You're Just Another Part Of Me . . .

A Rather Nation
Fulfill The Truth
The Final Message
We're Bring To You
There Is No Danger
Fulfill The Truth
So Come Together
We're Mean Is You

We're Sendin' Out
A Major Love
And This Is Our
Message To You
(Message To You)
The Planets Are Linin' Up
We're Bringin' Brighter Days
They're All In Line
Waitin' For You
So Look The Truth
You're Just Another Part Of Me . .

We're Sendin' Out
A Major Love
And This Is Our
Message To You
(Message To You)
The Planets Are Linin' Up
We're Bringin' Brighter Days
They're All In Line
Waitin' For You
Can't You See . . . ?
You're Just Another Part Of Me
Another Part Of Me . . .

We're Takin' Over
This Is The Truth, Baby
Another Part Of Me

BAD

I Just Can't Stop Loving You

Your Butt Is Mine
(Michael) Each Time The Wind Blows
I Hear Your Voice So I Call Your Name . . .
Whispers At Morning Our Love Is Dawning
Heaven's Glad You Came . . .
You Know How I Feel
This Thing Can't Go Wrong
I'm So Proud To Say I Love You
Your Love's Got Me High I Long To Get By
This Time Is Forever Love Is The Answer

(Siedah) I Hear Your Voice Now
You Are My Choice Now
The Love You Bring
Heaven's In My Heart
At Your Call I Hear Harps,
And Angels Sing
You Know How I Feel
This Thing Can't Go Wrong
I Can't Live My Life Without You

(Michael) I Just Can't Hold On
(Siedah) I Feel We Belong
(Michael) My Life Ain't Worth Living
If I Can't Be With You

(Both) I Just Can't Stop Loving You
I Just Can't Stop Loving You
And If I Stop . . .
Then Tell Me Just What Will I Do

(Siedah) 'Cause I Just Can't Stop
Loving You
(Michael) At Night When The
Stars Shine I Pray In You I'll Find
A Love So True . . .

(Siedah) When Morning Awakes Me
Will You Come And Take Me
I'll Wait For You

(Michael) You Know How I Feel
I Won't Stop Until
I Hear Your Voice Saying "I Do"

(Siedah) "I Do" This Thing Can't Go Wrong
(Michael) This Feeling's So Strong
(Siedah) Well, My Life Ain't Worth Living

(Both) If I Can't Be With You
I Just Can't Stop Loving You
I Just Can't Stop Loving You
And If I Stop . . .
Then Tell Me, Just What Will I Do

(Michael) I Just Can't Stop Loving You
(Siedah) We Can Change All The World Tomorrow
(Michael) We Can Sing Songs Of Yesterday
(Siedah) I Can Say, Hey Farewell To Sorrow
(Michael) This Is My Life And I,
(Both) Want To See You For Always
I Just Can't Stop Loving You

(Siedah) No, Baby (Michael) Oh!
(Both) I Just Can't Stop Loving You
(Siedah) If I Can't Stop!
(Both) And If I Stop . . .
(Siedah) No
(Michael) Oh! Oh! Oh . . . Oh . . .
(Siedah) What Will I Do? Uh . . . Ooh . . .
(Then Tell Me, Just What Will I Do)

(Both) I Just Can't Stop Loving You
(Michael) Hee! Hee! Hee! Know I Do Girl!
(Both) I Just Can't Stop Loving You
(Michael) You Know I Do And If I Stop . . .
(Both) Then Tell Me, Just What Will I Do
(Both) I Just Can't Stop Loving You

Dirty Diana

You'll Never Make Me Stay
So Take Your Weight Off Of Me
I Know Your Every Move
So Won't You Just Let Me Be
I've Been Here Times Before
But I Was Too Blind To See
That You Seduce Every Man
This Time You Won't Seduce Me

She's Saying That's Ok
Hey Baby Do What You Please
I Have The Stuff That You Want
I Am The Thing That You Need
She Looked Me Deep In The Eyes
She's Touchin' Me So To Start
She Says There's No Turnin' Back
She Trapped Me In Her Heart

Dirty Diana, Nah
Dirty Diana, Nah
Dirty Diana, No
Dirty Diana
Let Me Be!

Oh No Oh No Oh No .

She Likes The Boys In The Band
She Knows When They Come To Town
Every Musician's Fan After
The Curtain Comes Down
She Waits At Backstage Doors
For Those Who Have Prestige
Who Promise Fortune And Fame, A Life
That's So Carefree
She's Saying That's Ok
Hey Baby Do What You Want
I'll Be Your Night Lovin' Thing
I'll Be The Freak You Can Taunt
And I Don't Care What You Say
I Want To Go Too Far
I'll Be Your Everything
If You Make Me A Star

Dirty Diana, Nah...

She Said I Have To Go Home
'Cause I'm Real Tired You See
But I Hate Sleepin' Alone
Why Don't You Come With Me
I Said My Baby's At Home
She's Probably Worried Tonight
I Didn't Call On The Phone To
Say That I'm Alright

Diana Walked Up To Me,
She Said I'm All Yours Tonight
At That I Ran To The Phone
Sayin' Baby I'm Alright
I Said But Unlock The Door,
Because I Forgot The Key,
She Said He's Not Coming Back
Because He's Sleeping With Me

Dirty Diana, Nah...
Dirty Diana . . .
Come On!
Come On!
Come On!
Come On!...

Smooth Criminal

As He Came Into The Window
It Was The Sound Of A Crescendo
He Came Into Her Apartment
He Left The Bloodstains On The Carpet
She Ran Underneath The Table
He Could See She Was Unable
So She Ran Into The Bedroom
She Was Struck Down, It Was Her Doom

Annie Are You Ok So, Annie Are You Ok
Are You Ok, Annie Annie Are You Ok
So, Annie Are You Ok Are You Ok, Annie
Annie Are You Ok So, Annie Are You Ok
Are You Ok, Annie Annie Are You Ok
So, Annie Are You Ok, Are You Ok, Annie

Annie Are You Ok
Will You Tell Us That You're Ok
There's A Sign In The Window
That He Struck You-A Crescendo Annie
He Came Into Your Apartment
He Left The Bloodstains On The Carpet
Then You Ran Into The Bedroom
You Were Struck Down It Was Your Doom

Annie Are You Ok So, Annie Are You Ok
Are You Ok Annie Annie Are You Ok
So, Annie Are You Ok Are You Ok Annie
Annie Are You Ok So, Annie Are You Ok
Are You Ok Annie You've Been Hit By
You've Been Hit By A Smooth Criminal

So They Came Into The Outway
It Was Sunday-What A Black Day
Mouth To Mouth Resuscitation
Sounding Heartbeats Intimidations

(Repeat)

Okay, I Want Everybody To
Clear The Area Right Now!

(Annie Are You Ok)
I Don't Know!
(Will You Tell Us, That You're Ok)
I Don't Know!
(There's A Sign In The Window)
I Don't Know!
(That He Struck You A Crescendo Annie)
I Don't Know!
(He Came Into Your Apartment)
I Don't Know!
(Left Bloodstains On The Carpet)
I Don't Know Why Baby!
(Then You Ran Into The Bedroom)
I Don't Know!
(You Were Struck Down
(It Was Your Doom-Annie!)
(Annie Are You Ok)
Dad Gone It-Baby!
(Will You Tell Us, That You're Ok)
Dad Gone It-Baby!
(There's A Sign In The Window)
Dad Gone It-Baby!
(That He Struck You-A Crescendo Annie)
Hoo! Hoo!
(He Came Into Your Apartment)
Dad Gone It!
(Left Bloodstains On The Carpet)
Hoo! Hoo! Hoo!

MAN IN THE MIRROR

I'm Gonna Make A Change, For Once In My Life
It's Gonna Feel Real Good, Gonna Make A Difference
Gonna Make It Right . . .

As I, Turn Up The Collar On My Favorite Winter Coat
This Wind Is Blowin' My Mind, I See The Kids In The Street,
With Not Enough To Eat Who Am I, To Be Blind?
Pretending Not To See Their Need
A Summer's Disregard, A Broken Bottle Top
And A One Man's Soul
They Follow Each Other On The Wind Ya' Know
'Cause They Got Nowhere To Go
That's Why I Want You To Know

I'm Starting With The Man In The Mirror
I'm Asking Him To Change His Ways
And No Message Could Have Been Any Clearer
If You Wanna Make The World A Better Place
Take A Look At Yourself, And Then Make A Change
(Na Na Na, Na Na Na, Na Na, Na Nah)

I've Been A Victim Of A Selfish Kind Of Love
It's Time That I Realize
There Are Some With No Home, Not A Nickel To Loan
Could It Be Really Me, Pretending That They're Not Alone?

A Willow Deeply Scarred, Somebody's Broken Heart
And A Washed-Out Dream (Washed-Out Dream)
They Follow The Pattern Of The Wind, Ya' See
Cause They Got No Place To Be
That's Why I'm Starting With Me

I'm Starting With The Man In The Mirror
I'm Asking Him To Change His Ways
And No Message Could Have Been Any Clearer
If You Wanna Make The World A Better Place
Take A Look At Yourself And Then Make A Change

I'm Starting With The Man In The Mirror
I'm Asking Him To Change His Ways
And No Message Could Have Been Any Clearer
If You Wanna Make The World A Better Place
Take A Look At Yourself And Then Make That Change

I'm Starting With The Man In The Mirror,
I'm Asking Him To Change His Ways
No Message Could Have Been Any Clearer
If You Wanna Make The World A Better Place
Take A Look At Yourself And Then Make The Change
You Gotta Get It Right, While You Got The Time
'Cause When You Close Your Heart You Can't Close Your
Your Mind Then You Close Your Mind!
That Man, That Man, That Man That Man
With That Man In The Mirror

That Man, That Man, That Man
I'm Asking Him To Change His Ways
You Know That Man No Message Could Have
Been Any Clearer If You Wanna Make The World
A Better Place Take A Look At Yourself And
Then Make A Change Hoo! Hoo! Hoo! Hoo! Hoo!
Na Na Na, Na Na Na, Na Na,

Gonna Feel Real Good Now!
Yeah Yeah! Yeah Yeah! Yeah Yeah!
Na Na Na, Na Na Na, Na Na, Na Nah
Oh No, No No I'm Gonna Make A Change
It's Gonna Feel Real Good! Come On!
Just Lift Yourself You Know You've Got To
Stop It. Yourself! I've Got To Make That
Change, Today! Hoo! You Got To You Got
To Not Let Yourself Brother Hoo!
You Know I've Got To Get That Man, That Man
You've Got To You've Got To Move! Come
On! Come On! You Got To Stand Up! Stand Up!
Stand Up! Stand Up And Lift Yourself, Now!
Hoo! Hoo! Hoo! Aaow!
Gonna Make That Change Come On!
You Know It! You Know It! You Know It!

BAD

Leave Me Alone

I Don't Care What You Talkin' 'Bout Baby
I Don't Care What You Say
Don't You Come Walkin'
Beggin' Back Mama
I Don't Care Anyway
Time After Time I Gave You All Of My Money
No Excuses To Make
Ain't No Mountain That I
Can't Climb Baby
All Is Going My Way

'Cause There's A Time When You're Right
And You Know You Must Fight
Who's Laughing Baby, Don't
You Know
And There's The Choice That We Make
And This Choice You Will Take
Who's Laughin' Baby?

So Just Leave Me Alone
Leave Me Alone Leave Me Alone
Leave Me Alone Leave Me Alone
Leave Me Alone Leave Me Alone-Stop It!
Just Stop Doggin' Me Around
Just Stop Doggin' Me

There Was A Time I Used To
Say Girl I Need You
But Who Is Sorry Now
You Really Hurt, You Used To
Take And Deceive Me
Now Who Is Sorry Now
You Got A Way Of Making Me
Feel So Sorry
I Found Out Right Away
Don't You Come Walkin'-
Beggin' I Ain't Lovin' You
Don't You Get In My Way 'Cause
There's A Time When You're Right
And You Know You Must Fight
Who's Laughing Baby-Don't You Know?
And There's The Choice That We Make
And This Choice You Will Take
Who's Laughin' Baby?

[Repeat]
So Just Leave Me Alone
Leave Me Alone Leave Me Alone
Leave Me Alone Leave Me Alone
Leave Me Alone Leave Me Alone
Stop It!
Just Stop Doggin' Me Around
Leave Me Alone
Leave Me Alone
Leave Me Alone
Leave Me Alone
(Leave Me Alone
Leave Me Alone-Stop It!

Just Stop Doggin' Me Around
Just Stop Doggin' Me
Don't Come Beggin' Me
Don't Come Beggin'
Don't Come Lovin' Me
Don't Come Beggin'
I Love You
I Don't Want It
I Don't . . .
I Don't . . .
I . . .I . . . Aaow!
Hee Hee!
Don't Come Beggin' Me
Don't Come Beggin'
Don't Come Lovin' Me
Don't Come Beggin'
I Love You
I Don't Want It
I Don't Need It

Streetwalker (2001)

Pretty Baby Kisses For Your Loving
I Really Get It When You're
Next To Me Yeah Yeah
I'm So Excited How You
Give Me All Your Loving
I Got It Coming And It's Ecstacy
Streetwalking Baby

Cause Everyday I Watch You
Paint The Town So Pretty
I See You Coming In And Off
On My Thought Yeah Yeah
You Don't Believe Me Then
You Can Ask My Brother
Cause Everyday At Six
Home Alone

Because
Baby I Love You Baby I Love You
Baby I Love You Baby I Love You me
Baby I Love You You're So Satisfying

I Hear You Walking
Cause Your Body's Talking To Me
I Chase You Every Step Of The Way Yeah Yeah
An Invitation To Some
Faraway Hot Island
If I Can Show You Baby
Home With Me

You See I Never Met A Girl
Just Like You Come So Easy
Don't You Break My Heart
Cause I Love You

You See I Never Met A Girl
Just Like You Come So Easy
Don't You Break My Heart
Cause I Love You
Streetwalking Baby

Why Don't You Give Me Some Time
Won't You Give Me Some Time
Why Don't You Give Me Some Time
Won't You Give Me Some Time

I have to tell you
That you give me strong hot fever
My every thought is you
And that's a fact yeah yeah
I'd like to take you places
How about New York City
Or Paris, France
What do you think of that

[Repeat]
Streetwalking Baby
I got it coming baby

Baby I Love You Baby I love you
Baby I Want You Baby Come Love Me
Love Me Baby
Got To Have Some Loving
Got To Make You Mine
Got To Give Some Loving
Gonna Give You Loving
Make You Mine
Got To Get Your Love
Got To Give Some Love
Got To Make Somebody
I Told You I Told You

Fly Away (2001)

Our love's in motion
Give me a notion 'cause
You know we'll never part
Our love goodbye

I love in season
Give me a reason 'cause
You know we'll never part
Our love goodbye

And together we'll fly
I'll give you my heart
No place too far for us
We don't need it...

Baby don't make me
Baby don't make me
Baby don't make me
Fly Away Gonna stay
Love today

Baby don't make me
Baby don't make me
Baby don't make me
Fly Away Gonna stay
Love today...

I love a notion
Give me a motion 'cause
You know we'll never see
The thing you see

I love a reason
Give me a treason 'cause
You know we'll never part
I love so hard

And together we'll fly
I'll give you my heart
(I'll give you my heart)
No place too far for us
We don't need it...

[Repeat]

Love is here to stay...

You know baby
I don't wanna go away
I don't wanna fly away
Oh no...

Alone at last
I give you my heart
(I give you my heart)
No place too far for us
We don't need it...

[Repeat]

Love you
Love you
Love you girl...
Make me fly away...

DANGEROUS

Jam

Nation To Nation All The World
Must Come Together Face The Problems
That We See Then Maybe Somehow
We Can Work It Out
I Asked My Neighbor
For A Favor She Said Later
What Has Come Of
All The People Have We Lost Love
Of What It's About

I Have To Find My Peace Cuz
No One Seems To Let Me Be
False Prophets Cry Of Doom
What Are The Possibilities
I Told My Brother
There'll Be Problems,
Times And Tears For Fears,
We Must Live Each Day
Like It's The Last

Go With It Go With It Jam
It Ain't Too Much Stuff
It Ain't Too Much
It Ain't Too Much For Me To
Jam It Ain't
It Ain't Too Much Stuff
It Ain't Don't You
It Ain't Too Much For Me To

The World Keeps Changing
Rearranging Minds
And Thoughts
Predictions Fly Of Doom
The Baby Boomers
Has Come Of Age
We'll Work It Out

I Told My Brothers
Don't You Ask Me
For No Favors
I'm Conditioned By
The System
Don't You Talk To Me
Don't Scream And Shout

She Pray To God, To Buddha
Then She Sings A
Talmud Song
Confusions Contradict
The Self Do We Know Right
From Wrong I Just Want You To
Recognize Me In The Temple
You Can't Hurt Me
I Found Peace Within Myself

Go With It Go With It
Jam
It Ain't It Ain't Too Much Stuff
It Ain't Too Much
It Ain't Too Much For Me To Jam
It Ain't It Ain't Too Much Stuff
It Ain't Too Much
It Ain't Too Much For Me Jam...

Jam (cont)

[Rap Performed By Heavy D]
Jam Jam
Here Comes The Man
Hot Damn
The Big Boy Stands
Movin' Up A Hand
Makin' Funky Tracks
With My Man
Michael Jackson
Smooth Criminal
That's The Man
Mike's So Relaxed
Mingle Mingle Jingle
In The Jungle
Bum Rushed The Door
3 And 4's In A Bundle
Execute The Plan
First I Cooled Like A Fan
Got With Janet
Then With Guy
Now With Michael
Cause It Ain't Hard To...

Jam It Ain't
It Ain't Too Much Stuff
It Ain't Too Much
It Ain't Too Much For Me To
Jam Get On It
It Ain't Too Much Stuff
It Ain't Don't Stop
It Ain't Too Much For Me To
Jam It Ain't
It Ain't Too Much Stuff
It Ain't Don't You
It Ain't Too Much For Me To
Jam It Ain't
It Ain't Too Much Stuff
It Ain't Don't You
It Ain't Too Much For Me To

It Ain't Too Hard For Me
To Jam [9x]
Get On It Jam
It Ain't It Ain't Too Much Stuff
It Ain't Don't You
It Ain't Too Much For Me To
Jam It Ain't Too Much Stuff
It Ain't Too Much
It Ain't Too Much For Me To
Jam It Ain't Too Much Stuff
It Ain't Too Much
It Ain't Too Much For Me To
Jam Too Much
It Ain't Too Much Stuff
It Ain't Don't You
It Ain't Too Much For Me To

Get On It
Get On It
Give It Baby
Give It To Me
Come On
You Really Give It Too Me
Got To Give It
You Just Want To Give It

Why You Wanna Trip On Me

They Say I'm Different
They Don't Understand
But There's A Bigger Problem
That's Much More In Demand
You Got World Hunger
Not Enough To Eat
So There's Really No Time
To Be Trippin' On Me

You Got School Teachers
Who Don't Wanna Teach
You Got Grown People
Who Can't Write Or Read
You Got Strange Diseases
Ah But There's No Cure
You Got Many Doctors
That Aren't So Sure
So Tell Me

Why You Wanna Trip On Me
Why You Wanna Trip On Me
Stop Trippin'

We've Got More Problems
Than We'll Ever Need
You Got Gang Violence
And Bloodshed On The Street
You Got Homeless People
With No Food To Eat
With No Clothes On Their Back
And No Shoes For Their Feet

We've Got Drug Addiction
In The Minds Of The Weak
We've Got So Much Corruption
Police Brutality
We've Got Streetwalkers
Walkin' Into Darkness
Tell Me
What Are We Doin'

To Try To Stop This

Why You Wanna Trip On Me
Why You Wanna Trip On Me
Why You Wanna Trip On Me
Why You Wanna Trip On Me
Ooh Stop Trippin'
Yeah Stop Trippin'
Everybody Just Stop Trippin'

Why You Wanna Trip On Me
Why You Wanna Trip On Me
Why You Wanna Trip On Me
Why You Wanna Trip On Me
Stop Trippin'

Why You Wanna Trip On Me
Why You Wanna Trip On Me
Why You Wanna Trip On Me
Why You Wanna Trip On Me
Ooh Stop Trippin'
Yeah Stop Trippin'
Everybody Just Stop Trippin'

Stop Trippin'
Stop Trippin'
Stop Trippin'
Stop Trippin'

DANGEROUS

In The Closet

(Princess Stephanie of Monaco)
There's Something
I Have To Say To You
If You Promise You'll
Understand
I Cannot Contain Myself
When In Your Presence
I'm So Humble
Touch Me
Don't Hide Our Love
Woman To Man

(Michael) She's Just A Lover
Who's Doin' Me By
It's Worth The Giving
It's Worth The Try
You Cannot Cleave It
Or Put It In The Furnace
You Cannot Wet It
You Cannot Burn It

She Wants To Give It
(She Wants To Give It)
(Aahh, She Wants To Give It)
Dare Me
(She Wants To Give It)
(Aahh, She Wants To Give It)
She Wants To Give It
(She Wants To Give It)
(Aahh, She Wants To Give It)
(She Wants To Give It)
(Aahh, She Wants To Give It)

(Princess Stephanie of Monaco)
One Thing In Life
You Must Understand
The Truth Of Lust
Woman To Man
So Open The Door
And You Will See
There Are No Secrets
Make Your Move
Set Me Free

(Michael) Because There's Something
About You Baby
That Makes Me Want
To Give It To You
I Swear There's Something
About You Baby

Just Promise Me
Whatever We Say
Or Whatever We Do
To Each Other
For Now We'll Make A Vow
To Just
Keep It In The Closet

If You Can Get It
It's Worth A Try
I Really Want It
I Can't Deny
It's Just Desire
I Really Love It

In The Closet (cont)

(Princess Stephanie of Monaco)
'Cause If It's Aching
You Have To Rub It

She Wants To Give It
(She Wants To Give It)
(Aahh, She Wants To Give It)
(She Wants To Give It)
(Aahh, She Wants To Give It)
She Wants To Give It
(She Wants To Give It)
(Aahh, She Wants To Give It)
(She Wants To Give It)
(Aahh, She Wants To Give It)

(Princess Stephanie of Monaco)
Just Open The Door
And You Will See
This Passion Burns
Inside Of Me
Don't Say To Me
You'll Never Tell
Touch Me There
Make The Move
Cast The Spell

(Michael) Because There's Something
About You Baby
That Makes Me Want
To Give It To You
I Swear There's Something
About You Baby
That Makes Me Want

Just Promise Me
Whatever We Say
Or Do To Each Other
For Now We'll Make
A Vow To Just
Keep It In The Closet

Because There's Something
About You Baby
That Makes Me Want
To Give It To You
Because There's Something
About You Baby
That Makes Me Want
To Give It To You
Because There's Something
About You Baby
That Makes Me Want
To Give It To You
Because There's Something
About You Baby
That Makes Me Want
To Give It To You

Just Promise Me
Whatever We Say
Or Do To Each Other
For Now We'll Make
A Vow To Just
Keep It In The Closet

She Drives Me Wild

She's Got The Look
She's So Fine
And You Know Damn Well
The Girl Will Be Mine

She's Got The Breaks
She's The Scene
And You Know Damn Well
She Gives It To Me

Black Jeans And
A Turtleneck Sweater
I Know The Girl
Is Fakin' 'Cause
I've Seen Her Look Better

She's Composition
She's Statistical Fact
She Got It Ready
For The Willing
Got It Kicking Of The Back

She's Got The Look
She's Got The Look
Wanna Know Better
She's Got The Look
She's Driving Me Wild

She's Got The Look
Wanna Know Better
She's Got The Look
She's Driving Me Wild

Come To The Place
Shock To See
And You Know Damn Well
You Know What I Mean
Hot In The Face
One And 3

Like A Pleasure Trip
Like You've Never Seen
Satin Lace
And A Paisley Cut Top
The Girl Is Wasting Over
And She Knows
She's Got

She's Got Position
She's Got Just What It Takes

Got A Mojo
In Her Pocket
Got It Ready
Just In Case

She's Got The Look
Wanna Know Better
She's Got The Look
She's Driving Me Wild

She's Got The Look
Wanna Know Better
She's Got The Look
She's Driving Me Wild

(Rap)
She's Got The Look...

DANGEROUS

Remember The Time

Do You Remember
When We Fell In Love
We Were Young
And Innocent Then
Do You Remember
How It All Began
It Just Seemed Like Heaven
So Why Did It End?

Do You Remember Back In The Fall
We'd Be Together All Day Long
Do You Remember Us Holding Hands
In Each Other's Eyes We'd Stare

Do You Remember The Time
When We Fell In Love
Do You Remember The Time
When We First Met Girl
Do You Remember The Time
When We Fell In Love
Do You Remember The Time

Do You Remember
How We Used To Talk
We'd Stay On The Phone
At Night Till Dawn
Do You Remember
All The Things We Said
Like I Love You So
I'll Never Let You Go

Do You Remember Back In The Spring
Every Morning Birds Would Sing
Do You Remember
Those Special Times
They'll Just Go On And On
In The Back Of My Mind

Do You Remember The Time
When We Fell In Love
Do You Remember The Time
When We First Met Girl
Do You Remember The Time
When We Fell In Love
Do You Remember The Time
Those Sweet Memories
Will Always Be Dear To Me
And Girl No Matter What Was Said
I Will Never Forget What We Had
Now Baby

(repeat)

Remember The Times Ooh
Do You Remember Girl

On The Phone You And Me
Till Dawn, Two Or Three
What About Us Girl

Do You, Do You, Do You,
Do You, Do You
In The Park, On The Beach
You And Me In Spain
What About, What About...

Ooh... In The Park
After Dark..., Do You, Do You, Do You
Do You, Do You, Do You, Do You
Yeah Yeah Who

Can't Let Her Get Away

I Thought She Had To Have It
Since The First Time She Came
Who Knows The Situation
Mysteries Do Remain
And Now I Wonder Why
I Breakdown When I Cry
Is It Something I Said
Or Is It Just A Lie
Is It Just A Lie

I Try So Hard To Love You
Some Things Take
Time And Shame
I Think The Whole World
Of You
Your Thoughts Of Me Remain
I'll Play The Fool For You
I'll Change The Rules For You
Just Say It And I'll Do
Just Make This Thing Come True
Make A Dream Come True

If I Let Her Get Away
Though I'm Begging
On My Knees
I'll Be Crying Everyday
Knowing The Girl
That Got Away

I Can't Let
I Can't Let Her Get Away
I Can't Let
I Can't Let Her Get Away

I Can't Let
I Can't Let Her Get Away
I Can't Let
I Can't Let Her Get Away

I Tried To Mastermind It
By Saying Let You Be
But Everytime I Did It
The Hurt Came Back At Me
I Told You That I Need You
A Thousand Times And Why
I Played The Fool For You
And Still You Said Goodbye
Still You Said Goodbye

If I Let Her Get Away
Then The World Will
Have To See
A Fool Who Lives Alone
The Fool Who
Set You Free

I Can't Let
I Can't Let Her Get Away
I Can't Let
I Can't Let Her Get Away...

Black Or White

I Took My Baby
On A Saturday Bang
Boy Is That Girl With You
Yes We're One And The Same

Now I Believe In Miracles
And A Miracle
Has Happened Tonight

But, If You're Thinkin'
About My Baby
It Don't Matter If You're
Black Or White

They Print My Message
In The Saturday Sun
I Had To Tell Them
I Ain't Second To None

And I Told About Equality
An It's True
Either You're Wrong Or You're Right

But, If You're Thinkin' About My Baby
It Don't Matter If You're
Black Or White

I Am Tired Of This Devil
I Am Tired Of This Stuff
I Am Tired Of This Business
Sew When The Going Gets Rough
I Ain't Scared Of Your Brother
I Ain't Scared Of No Sheets
I Ain't Scare Of Nobody
Girl When The Goin' Gets Mean

(L. T. B. Rap Performance)
Protection For Gangs, Clubs
And Nations Causing Grief In
Human Relations
It's A Turf War On A Global Scale
I'd Rather Hear Both Sides
Of The Tale See, It's Not About
Races Just Places Faces
Where Your Blood Comes From
Is Where Your Space Is
I've Seen The Bright Get Duller
I'm Not Going To Spend
My Life Being A Color

Don't Tell Me You Agree With Me
When I Saw You Kicking
Dirt In My Eye

But, If You're Thinkin' About
My Baby It Don't Matter If You're
Black Or White

I Said If You're Thinkin' Of
Being My Baby
It Don't Matter If
You're Black Or White

I Said If You're Thinkin' Of
Being My Brother
It Don't Matter If You're
Black Or White

It's Black, It's White
It's Tough For You To Get By

DANGEROUS

Heal The World

There's A Place In
Your Heart
And I Know That It Is Love
And This Place Could
Be Much
Brighter Than Tomorrow
And If You Really Try
You'll Find There's No Need
To Cry
In This Place You'll Feel
There's No Hurt Or Sorrow

There Are Ways
To Get There
If You Care Enough
For The Living
Make A Little Space
Make A Better Place...

Heal The World
Make It A Better Place
For You And For Me
And The Entire Human Race
There Are People Dying
If You Care Enough
For The Living
Make A Better Place
For You And For Me

If You Want To Know Why
There's A Love That
Cannot Lie
Love Is Strong
It Only Cares For
Joyful Giving
If We Try
We Shall See
In This Bliss
We Cannot Feel
Fear Or Dread
We Stop Existing And
Start Living

Then It Feels That Always
Love's Enough For
Us Growing
So Make A Better World
Make A Better World...

Heal The World
Make It A Better Place
For You And For Me
And The Entire Human Race
There Are People Dying
If You Care Enough
For The Living
Make A Better Place
For You And For Me

And The Dream We Were
Conceived In
Will Reveal A Joyful Face
And The World We
Once Believed In
Will Shine Again In Grace
Then Why Do We Keep
Strangling Life
Wound This Earth
Crucify Its Soul
Though It's Plain To See
This World Is Heavenly

We Could Fly So High
Let Our Spirits Never Die
In My Heart
I Feel You Are All
My Brothers
Create A World With
No Fear
Together We'll Cry
Happy Tears
See The Nations Turn
Their Swords
Into Plowshares

We Could Really Get There
If You Cared Enough
For The Living
Make A Little Space
To Make A Better Place...

Heal The World
Make It A Better Place
For You And For Me
And The Entire Human Race
There Are People Dying
If You Care Enough
For The Living
Make A Better Place
For You And For Me

Heal The World
Make It A Better Place
For You And For Me
And The Entire Human Race
There Are People Dying
If You Care Enough
For The Living
Make A Better Place
For You And For Me

Heal The World
Make It A Better Place
For You And For Me
And The Entire Human Race
There Are People Dying
If You Care Enough
For The Living
Make A Better Place
For You And For Me

There Are People Dying
If You Care Enough
For The Living
Make A Better Place
For You And For Me

There Are People Dying
If You Care Enough
For The Living
Make A Better Place
For You And For Me

You And For Me
You And For Me
You And For Me
You And For Me
You And For Me
You And For Me
You And For Me

DANGEROUS

Who Is It

I Gave Her Money
I Gave Her Time
I Gave Her Everything
Inside One Heart Could Find
I Gave Her Passion
My Very Soul
I Gave Her Promises
And Secrets So Untold

And She Promised Me Forever
And A Day We'd Live As One
We Made Our Vows
We'd Live A Life Anew
And She Promised Me In Secret
That She'd Love Me For All Time
It's A Promise So Untrue
Tell Me What Will I Do?

And It Doesn't Seem To Matter
And It Doesn't Seem Right
'Cause The Will Has Brought
No Fortune
Still I Cry Alone At Night
Don't You Judge Of My Composure
'Cause I'm Lying To Myself
And The Reason Why She Left Me
Did She Find In Someone Else?

(Who Is It?)
It Is A Friend Of Mine
(Who Is It?)
Is It My Brother!
(Who Is It?)
Somebody Hurt My Soul, Now
(Who Is It?)
I Can't Take This Stuff No More

I Am The Damned
I Am The Dead
I Am The Agony Inside
The Dying Head
This Is Injustice
Woe Unto Thee
I Pray This Punishment
Would Have Mercy On Me

And She Promised Me Forever
That We'd Live Our Life As One
We Made Our Vows
We'd Live A Love So True
It Seems That She Has Left Me
For Such Reasons Unexplained
I Need To Find The Truth
But See What Will I Do!

And It Doesn't Seem To Matter
And It Doesn't Seem Right
'Cause The Will Has Brought
No Fortune
Still I Cry Alone At Night
Don't You Judge Of My Composure
'Cause I'm Bothered Everyday
And She Didn't Leave A Letter
She Just Up And Ran Away

(Who Is It?) It Is A Friend Of Mine
(Who Is It?) Is It My Brother?
(Who Is It?) Somebody Hurt My Soul, Now
(Who Is It?)
I Can't Take It 'Cause I'm Lonely

Give In To Me

She Always Takes It With A Heart
Of Stone 'Cause All She Does Is
Throw It Back To Me
I've Spent A Lifetime
Looking For Someone
Don't Try To Understand Me
Just Simply Do The Things I Say

Love Is A Feeling Give It When
 I Want It 'Cause I'm On Fire
Quench My Desire
Give It When I Want It
Talk To Me Woman
Give In To Me Give In To Me

You Always Knew Just How To
Make Me Cry And Never Did I
Ask You Questions Why
It Seems You Get Your Kicks From
Hurting Me Don't Try To
Understand Me Because Your Words
Just Aren't Enough

Love Is A Feeling Quench My
Desire Give It When I Want It
Takin' Me Higher Love Is A Woman
I Don't Wanna Hear It
Give In To Me Give In To Me

You And Your Friends
Were Laughing At Me In Town
But It's Okay And It's Okay
You Wont Be Laughing Girl
When I'm Not Around
I'll Be Okay And I'll, I'll Not Find
Gotta, The Peace Of Mind No

Don't Try To Tell Me Because Your
Words Just Aren't Enough

Love Is A Feeling Quench My
Desire Give It When I Want It
Takin' Me Higher
Talk To Me Woman
Love Is A Feeling Give In To Me
Give In To Me Give In To Me

Love Is A Feeling
I Don't Wanna Hear It
Quench My Desire
Takin' Me Higher
Tell It To The Preacher
Satisfy The Feeling
Give In To Me Give In To Me

I Don't Wanna I Don't Wanna
I Don't Wanna Hear It Give It
To The Fire Talk To Me Woman
Quench My Desire I Don't Like
A Lady Talk To Me Baby
Give In To Me

Give In To The Fire Give In To Me
Give In To Me Give In To Me

Love Is A Woman Give In To Me
Give In To Me Give In To Me
Give In To Me

'Cause I'm On Fire Talk To Me

Will You Be There

Hold Me
Like The River Jordan
And I Will Then Say To Thee
You Are My Friend

Carry Me
Like You Are My Brother
Love Me Like A Mother
Will You Be There?

Weary
Tell Me Will You Hold Me
When Wrong, Will You Scold Me
When Lost Will You Find Me?

But They Told Me
A Man Should Be Faithful
And Walk When Not Able
And Fight Til The End
But I'm Only Human

Everyone's Taking Control Of Me
Seems That The World's
Got A Role For Me
I'm So Confused
Will You Show To Me
You'll Be There For Me
And Care Enough To Bear Me

(Hold Me) (Lay Your Head Lowly)
(Softly Then Boldly) (Carry Me There)

(Lead Me) (Love Me And Feed Me)
(Kiss Me And Free Me)
(I Will Feel Blessed)

(Carry) (Carry Me Boldly)
(Lift Me Up Slowly) (Carry Me There)

(Save Me) (Heal Me And Bathe Me)
(Softly You Say To Me)
(I Will Be There)

(Lift Me) (Lift Me Up Slowly)
(Carry Me Boldly)
(Show Me You Care)

(Hold Me) (Lay Your Head Lowly)
(Softly Then Boldly)
(Carry Me There)

(Need Me) (Love Me And Feed Me)
(Kiss Me And Free Me)
(I Will Feel Blessed)

In Our Darkest Hour
In My Deepest Despair
Will You Still Care?
Will You Be There?
In My Trials
And My Tribulations
Through Our Doubts
And Frustrations
In My Violence
In My Turbulence
Through My Fear
And My Confessions
In My Anguish And My Pain
Through My Joy And My Sorrow
In The Promise Of Another Tomorrow

DANGEROUS

Keep The Faith

If You Call Out Loud
Will It Get Inside
Through The Heart Of Your Surrender
To Your Alibis
And You Can Say The Words
Like You Understand
But The Power's In Believing
So Give Yourself
A Chance

* 'Cause You Can
Climb The Highest Mountain
Swim The Deepest Sea, Hee
All You
Need Is The Will To Want It
And Uhh, Little Self-Esteem

So Keep The Faith
Don't Let Nobody Turn You 'Round
You Gotta Know When It's Good To Go
To Get Your Dreams
Up Off The Ground
Keep The Faith, Baby, Yea
Because It's Just
A Matter Of Time
Before Your Confidence Will Win Out
Believe In Yourself
No Matter What It's Gon' Take
You Can Be A Winner
But You Got
To Keep The Faith
...Gon' Keep It Brother
You Got It *

And When You Think Of Trust
Does It Lead You Home
To A Place That You Only Dream Of
When You're All Alone
And You Can Go
By Feel 'Stead Of Circumstance
But The Power's In Believing
So Give Yourself A Chance
I Know That You Can Sail Across
The Water Float Across The Sky, High
Any Road That You Take
Will Get You There
If You Only Try
So Keep The Faith, Ow
Don't Let Nobody Take You Down,
Brother Just Keep Your Eyes On The
Prize And Your Feet
Flat On The Ground

Keep The Faith, Baby, Yea
Because It's Just A Matter Of Time
Before Your Confidence Will Win Out
I Told My Brother How To Do
The Thing Right Lift Up Your
Head And Show
The World You Got Pride
Go For What You Want
Don't Let 'Em Get In Your Way
You Can Be A Winner
But You Got To Keep The Faith
Gon' Keep It Brother You Got It

I Know That Keepin' The Faith
Means Never Givin' Up On Love
But The Power That Love Has To
Make It Right Makes It Makes It Right

Keep The Faith (cont)

Don't Let Nobody Turn You '
Round Brother You Got To
Know When It's Good To Go
To Get Your Dreams Up Off
The Ground Keep The Faith
Baby, Yea Because It's Just A
Matter Of Time Before Your
Confidence Will Win Out
Better Stand Up And Act Like You
Wanna Do Right Don't Play The
Fool For The Rest Of Your Life
Work On It Brother And You'll
Make It Someday Go For What
You Want And Don't Forget The
Faith Look At Yourself
And What You Doin' Right Now
Stand Back A Minute
Just To Check Yourself Out
Straighten Out Your Life
And How You're Livin' Each Day
Get Yourself Together
'Cause You Got To Keep The Faith
Uh, Uh, Uh

Don't Let Nobody Take You Down,
Brother
Just Keep Your Eyes On The Prize
And Your Feet Flat On The Ground
Keep The Faith, Baby, Yea
Because It's Just A Matter Of Time
Before Your Confidence
Will Win Out Lift Up Your Mind
Before Your Mind Gets Blown
Some Things In Life
You Best Just Leave Them Alone
Go For What You Want
Don't Let It Get In Your Way
You Can Make It Happen
But Ya Got Ta Keep The Faith
Gon' Keep It Brother
You Got To Keep The Faith
Yeah Keep The Faith
Gon' Keep It Sister
You Got To Keep The Faith
Now, Now
I'll Show My Brotha
How To Do The Thing Right
Lift Up Your Head
And Show The World
You Got Pride
Go For What You Want
Don't Let 'Em Get In Your Way
You Can Be A Winner
If You Keep The Faith
Straighten Out Yourself
And Get Your Mind On Track
Dust Off Your Butt
And Get Your Self-Respect Back
You've Known Me Long Enough
To Know That I Don't Play
Take It Like You Want It
But You Got To Keep The Faith Gon'
Don't Let Nobody Take You Down
Just Keep Your Eyes On The Prize
And Get Your Feet Back On
The Ground
Keep The Faith, Baby, Yea
Because It's Just
A Matter Of Time
Before Your Confidence Will Win Out

Dangerous

The Way She Came Into
The Place I Knew Right
Then And There There
Was Something Different
About This Girl

The Way She Moved
Her Hair, Her Face,
Her Lines Divinity In
Motion

As She Stalked The Room
I Could Feel The Aura
Of Her Presence
Every Head Turned
Feeling Passion And Lust

The Girl Was Persuasive
The Girl I Could Not Trust
The Girl Was Bad
The Girl Was Dangerous

I Never Knew But I Was
Walking The Line
Come Go With Me
I Said I Have No Time
And Don't You Pretend
We Didn't Talk On
The Phone My Baby Cried
She Left Me Standing Alone
She's So Dangerous
The Girl Is So Dangerous
Take Away My Money
Throw Away My Time
You Can Call Me Honey
But You're No Damn
Good For Me

She Came At Me In Sections
With The Eyes Of Desire
I Fell Trapped Into Her
Web Of Sin A Touch, A Kiss
A Whisper Of Love I Was At
The Point Of No Return

Deep In The Darkness Of
Passion's Insanity
I Felt Taken By Lust's
Strange Inhumanity
This Girl Was Persuasive
This Girl I Could Not Trust
The Girl Was Bad
The Girl Was Dangerous
I Never Knew
But I Was Living In Vain
She Called My House
She Said You Know My
Name And Don't You
Pretend You Never Did
Me Before With Tears
In Her Eyes My Baby
Walked Out The Door

She's So Dangerous
The Girl Is So Dangerous
Take Away My Money
Throw Away My Time
You Can Call Me Honey
But You're No Damn

Dangerous (cont)

Good For Me Dangerous
The Girl Is So Dangerous
I Have To Pray To God
'Cause I Know How
Lust Can Blind
It's A Passion In My Soul
But You're No Damn Lover
Friend Of Mine

I Can not Sleep Alone
Tonight My Baby Left
Me Here Tonight
I Cannot Cope 'Til It's
All Right You And Your
Manipulation
You Hurt My Baby

And Then It Happened
She Touched Me
For The Lips Of
A Strange Woman
Drop As A Honeycomb
And Her Mouth Was
Smoother Than Oil
But Her Inner Spirit And
Words Were As Sharp As
A Two-Edged Sword
But I Loved It
'Cause It's Dangerous

Dangerous
The Girl Is So Dangerous
Take Away My Money
Throw Away My Time
You Can Call Me Honey
But You're No Damn
Good For Me

Dangerous
The Girl Is So Dangerous
Take Away My Money
Throw Away My Time
You Can Call Me Honey
But You're No Damn Good
For Me

Dangerous
The Girl Is So Dangerous
Take Away My Money
Throw Away My Time
You Can Call Me Honey
But You're No Damn Good
For Me

Dangerous
The Girl Is So Dangerous
I Have To Pray To God
'Cause I Know How
Lust Can Blind
It's A Passion In My Soul
But You're No Damn Lover
Friend Of Mine
[Ad Libs Out]

HIStory - Past, Present And Future - Book 1

Scream

Tired Of Injustice
Tired Of The Schemes
Life Is Disgustin'
So What Does It Mean, Damnit
Kicking Me Down
I Got To Get Up
As Jacked As It Sounds
The Whole System Sucks, Damnit

Peek In The Shadow
Come Into The Light
You Tell Me I'm Wrong
Then You Better Prove You're Right
You're Sellin' Out Souls But
I Care About Mine
I've Got To Get Stronger
And I Won't Give Up The Fight

With Such Confusions
Don't It Make You Wanna Scream
(Make You Wanna Scream)
Your Bash Abusin'
Victimize Within The Scheme
You Try To Cope With Every Lie
They Scrutinize
Somebody Please Have Mercy
'Cause I Just Can't Take It

Stop Pressurin' Me
Just Stop Pressurin' Me
Stop Pressurin' Me
Make Me Wanna Scream
Stop Pressurin' Me
Just Stop Pressurin' Me
Stop Pressurin' Me
Make Me Wanna Scream

Tired Of Your Tellin'
(Tellin')
The Story Your Way
(The Story Your Way)
You're Causin' Confusion
(Confusion)
Then Think It's Okay, Damnit

Keep Changin' The Rules
While You're Playin' The Game
I Can't Take It Much Longer
I Think I Might Go Insane

(Now, Baby)
With Such Confusion
Don't It Make You Wanna Scream
(Make You Wanna Scream)
Your Bash Abusin'
Victimize Within The Scheme
(Scream It Baby)
You Find Your Pleasure
Scandalizin' Every Lie
Oh Father, Please Have Mercy
'Cause I Just Can't Take It

Stop Pressurin' Me
Just Stop Pressurin' Me
Stop Pressurin' Me
Make Me Wanna Scream

Scream (cont.)

Stop Pressurin' Me
Just Stop Pressurin' Me
Stop Fuckin' With Me
Make Me Wanna Scream

Oh, My God, Can't Believe What
I Saw As I Turned On The TV This
Evening I Was Disgusted By All The
Injustice All The Injustice
All The Injustice

Yeah Yeah
Baby

With Such Collusions
Don't It Make You Wanna Scream
(Make You Wanna Scream)
Your Bash Abusin'
(Make You Wanna Scream)
Victimize Within The Scheme
You Try To Cope With Every Lie
They Scrutinize
Oh Brother Please Have Mercy
'Cause I Just Can't Take It
Just Can't Take It

Stop Pressurin' Me
Just Stop Pressurin' Me
Stop Pressurin' Me
Make Me Wanna Scream
Stop Pressurin' Me
Just Stop Pressurin' Me
Stop Pressurin' Me
Make Me Wanna Scream

Stop Pressurin' Me
Just Stop Pressurin' Me
Stop Pressurin' Me
Make Me Wanna Scream
Stop Pressurin' Me
Just Stop Pressurin' Me
Stop Pressurin' Me
Make Me Wanna Scream

Stop Your Pressure!

They Don't Really About Us

Skin Head, Dead Head Everybody Gone Bad
Situation, Aggravation Everybody Allegation
In The Suite, On The News Everybody Dog Food
Bang Bang, Shot Dead Everybody's Gone Mad

All I Wanna Say Is That They Don't Really Care About Us
All I Wanna Say Is That They Don't Really Care About Us

Beat Me, Hate Me You Can Never Break Me
Will Me, Thrill Me You Can Never Kill Me
Jew Me, Sue Me Everybody Do Me
Kick Me, Kike Me Don't You Black Or White Me

All I Wanna Say Is That They Don't Really Care About Us
All I Wanna Say Is That They Don't Really Care About Us

Tell Me What Has Become Of My Life
I Have A Wife And Two Children Who Love Me
I Am The Victim Of Police Brutality, Now
I'm Tired Of Bein' The Victim Of Hate
You're Rapin' Me Of My Pride Oh, For God's Sake
I Look To Heaven To Fulfill Its Prophecy...
Set Me Free

Skin Head, Dead Head Everybody Gone Bad
Trepidation, Speculation Everybody Allegation
In The Suite, On The News Everybody Dog Food
Black Man, Black Male Throw Your Brother In Jail

All I Wanna Say Is That They Don't Really Care About Us
All I Wanna Say Is That They Don't Really Care About Us

Tell Me What Has Become Of My Rights
Am I Invisible Because You Ignore Me?
Your Proclamation Promised Me Free Liberty, Now
I'm Tired Of Bein' The Victim Of Shame
They're Throwing Me In A Class With A Bad Name
I Can't Believe This Is The Land From Which I Came
You Know I Do Really Hate To Say It
The Government Don't Wanna See
But If Roosevelt Was Livin'
He Wouldn't Let This Be, No, No
Skin Head, Dead Head Everybody Gone Bad
Situation, Speculation Everybody Litigation
Beat Me, Bash Me You Can Never Trash Me
Hit Me, Kick Me You Can Never Get Me

All I Wanna Say Is That They Don't Really Care About Us
All I Wanna Say Is That They Don't Really Care About Us

Some Things In Life They Just Don't Wanna See
But If Martin Luther Was Livin' He Wouldn't Let This Be

Skin Head, Dead Head Everybody Gone Bad
Situation, Segregation Everybody Allegation
In The Suite, On The News Everybody Dog Food
Kick Me, Strike Me Don't You Wrong Or Right Me

All I Wanna Say Is That They Don't Really Care About Us
All I Wanna Say Is That They Don't Really Care About Us

All I Wanna Say Is That They Don't Really Care About Us
All I Wanna Say Is That They Don't Really Care About Us

All I Wanna Say Is That They Don't Really Care About Us
All I Wanna Say Is That They Don't Really Care About Us

HIStory - Past, Present And Future - Book 1

Stranger In Moscow

I Was Wandering In The Rain
Mask Of Life, Feelin' Insane
Swift And Sudden Fall From Grace
Sunny Days Seem Far Away
Kremlin's Shadow Belittlin' Me
Stalin's Tomb Won't Let Me Be
On And On And On It Came
Wish The Rain Would Just Let Me

How Does It Feel (How Does It Feel)
How Does It Feel
How Does It Feel
When You're Alone
And You're Cold Inside

Here Abandoned In My Fame
Armageddon Of The Brain
KGB Was Doggin' Me
Take My Name And Just Let Me Be
Then A Begger Boy Called My Name
Happy Days Will Drown The Pain
On And On And On It Came
And Again, And Again, And Again...
Take My Name And Just Let Me Be

How Does It Feel
How Does It Feel
How Does It Feel
How Does It Feel
How Does It Feel
How Does It Feel
When You're Alone
And You're Cold Inside

How Does It Feel
(How Does It Feel)
How Does It Feel
How Does It Feel
How Does It Feel
(How Does It Feel Now)
How Does It Feel
How Does It Feel
When You're Alone
And You're Cold Inside

Like Stranger In Moscow
Like Stranger In Moscow
We're Talkin' Danger
We're Talkin' Danger, Baby
Like Stranger In Moscow
We're Talkin' Danger
We're Talkin' Danger, Baby
Like Stranger In Moscow
I'm Live In Lonely
I'm Live In Lonely, Baby
Stranger In Moscow

I'm Live In Lonely
I'm Live In Lonely, Baby
Stranger In Moscow

This Time Around

This Time Around I'll Never Get Bit Though
You Really Wanna Fix Me This Time Around
You're Making Me Sick Though You Really
Wanna Get Me Somebody's Out Somebody's
Out To Get Me They Really Wanna Fix Me,
Hit Me But This Time Around I'm Taking
No Shit Though You Really Wanna Get Me
You Really Wanna Get Me

He Really Thought He Really Had Had A
Hold On Me He Really Thought He Really
Had They Thought They Really Had Control
Of Me He Really Thought He Really Had
Control Of Me He Really Thought He Really
Had They Thought They Really Could Control Me

This Time Around I'll Never Get Bit Though
You Really Wanna Get Me This Time Around I'm
Taking No Shit Though You Really Wanna Fix Me
Somebody's Out Somebody's Out To Use Me
They Really Want To Use Me And Then Falsely
Accuse Me This Time Around They'll Take It
Like Spit 'Cause You Really Can't Control Me

You Know You Can't Control Me He Really
Thought He Really Had Had A Hold On Me He
Really Thought He Really Had They Thought They
Really Had Control Of Me He Really Thought
He Really Had A Hold On Me He Really
Thought He Really Had They Thought They Really
Had Control Of Me He Really Thought He Really Had
Had A Hold On Me He Really Thought
He Really Had They Thought They Really Had
Control Of Me He Really Thought He Really Had
A Hold On Me He Really Thought He Really Had
They Thought They Really Had Control Of Me

[Rap: The Notorious BIG]
Listen, I've Got Problems Of My Own
Flashin' Cameras, Taps On My Phone
Even In My Home I Ain't Safe As I Should Be
Things Always Missin' Maybe It Could Be My Friends
They Ain't Friends If They Robbin' Me Stoppin'
Me From Makin' A Profit, See Apology Shallow Like
The Ocean I Guess I'll Resort To Gun Totin'
If I Was Dead Broke And Smokin' I'd Probably Be By
My Lonesome I'm A Killer Nigga I Ain't Jokin'
Endo Smoke Got Me Choked And I'm Hopin'
The Fool Comes Slippin' So I Could Blow'em Open
This Time Around I Changed Up My Flow
Got Rid Of The Rocks Got Pitts By The Door
I've Raised Other Peoples To Watch My Back
Stay Away From Strangers So I Won't Slack
And I Know My Nigga Mike Like That Baby

This Time Around Yeah...
He Really Thought He Really Had
Control Of Me He Really Thought He Really Had
They Thought They Really Had Control Of Me
He Really Thought He Really Had
A Hold On Me He Really Thought He Really Had
They Thought They Really Had Control Of Me
He Really Thought He Really Had
Had A Hold On Me He Really Thought He Really
Had They Thought They Really Had Control Of Me
He Really Thought He Really Had Control Of Me
He Really Thought He Really Had They Thought
They Really Had Control Of Me He Really
Thought He Really Had A Hold On Me
He Really Thought He Really Had
They Thought They Really Had Control Of Me

Earth Song

What About Sunrise What About Rain
What About All The Things
That You Said We Were To Gain...
What About Killing Fields
Is There A Time
What About All The Things
That You Said Was Yours And Mine...
Did You Ever Stop To Notice
All The Blood We've Shed Before
Did You Ever Stop To Notice
The Crying Earth The Weeping Shores?

What Have We've Done To The World
Look What We've Done
What About All The Peace
That You Pledge Your Only Son...
What About Flowering Fields
Is There A Time
What About All The Dreams
That You Said Was Yours And Mine...
Did You Ever Stop To Notice
All The Children Dead From War
Did You Ever Stop To Notice
The Crying Earth The Weeping Shores

I Used To Dream
I Used To Glance Beyond The Stars
Now I Don't Know Where We Are
Although I Know We've Drifted Far

Hey, What About Yesterday
What About The Seas
The Heavens Are Falling Down
I Can't Even Breathe
What About Apathy
I Need You
What About Nature's Worth
It's Our Planet's Womb
What About Animals
We've Turned Kingdoms To Dust
What About Elephants
Have We Lost Their Trust
What About Crying Whales
We're Ravaging The Seas
What About Forest Trails
Burnt Despite Our Pleas
What About The Holy Land
Torn Apart By Creed
What About The Common Man
Can't We Set Him Free
What About Children Dying
Can't You Hear Them Cry
Where Did We Go Wrong
Someone Tell Me Why
What About Babies
What About The Days
What About All Their Joy
What About The Man
What About The Crying Man
What About Abraham
What About Death Again
Do We Give A Damn

Whoo Whoo Whoo Whoo
Whoo Whoo Whoo Whoo
Whoo Whoo Whoo Whoo
Whoo Whoo Whoo Whoo
Whoo Whoo Whoo Whoo

HIStory - Past, Present And Future - Book 1

D.S.

They Wanna Get My Ass
Dead Or Alive You Know
He Really Tried To Take Me
Down By Surprise I Bet He
Missioned With The CIA
He Don't Do Half What He Say

Dom Sheldon Is A Cold Man
Dom Sheldon Is A Cold Man
Dom Sheldon Is A Cold Man
Dom Sheldon Is A Cold Man

He Out Shock In Every Single Way
He'll Stop At Nothing Just To Get
His Political Say He Think He Bad
Cause He's BSTA I Bet He Never
Had A Social Life Anyway You
Think He Brother With The KKK?
I Bet His Mother Never Taught Him
Right Anyway He Want Your Vote
Just To Remain TA. He Don't Do
Half What He Say

Dom Sheldon Is A Cold Man
Dom Sheldon Is A Cold Man
Dom Sheldon Is A Cold Man
Dom Sheldon Is A Cold Man

Dom S. Sheldon Is A Cold Man
Dom Sheldon Is A Cold Man
Dom Sheldon Is A Cold Man
Dom Sheldon Is A Cold Man

Does He Send Letters To The FBI?
Did He Say To Either Do It Or Die?

Dom Sheldon Is A Cold Man
Dom Sheldon Is A Cold Man
Dom Sheldon Is A Cold Man
Dom Sheldon Is A Cold Man

Dom S. Sheldon Is A Cold Man
Dom Sheldon Is A Cold Man
Dom Sheldon Is A Cold Man
Dom Sheldon Is A Cold Man

Dom S. Sheldon Is A Cold Man

Money

Lie For It Spy For It Kill For It Die For It

So You Call It Trust But I Say It's Just
In The Devils Game Of Greed And Lust

They Don't Care They'd Do Me For The
Money They Don't Care They Use Me
For The Money

So You Go To Church Read The Holy Word
In The Scheme Of Life Its All Absurd

They Don't Care They'd Kill For The Money
Do Or Dare The Thrill For The Money

You're Saluting The Flag Your Country
Trusts You Now You're Wearing A Badge
You're Called The Just Few And You're
Fighting The Wars A Soldier Must Do I'll
Never Betray Or Deceive You My Friend But

If You Show Me The Cash Then I Will Take It
If You Tell Me To Cry Then I Will Fake It
If You Give Me A Hand Then I Will Shake It

You Do Anything For Money...

Anything Anything Anything For Money
Would Lie For You Would Die For You
Even Sell My Soul To The Devil

Anything Anything Anything For Money
Would Lie For You Would Die For You
Even Sell My Soul To The Devil

Insurance? Where Do Your Loyalties Lie?
Is That Your Alibi? I Don't Think So
You Don't Care You'd Do Her For The Money
Say Its Fair You Sue Her For The Money
Want Your Pot Of Gold Need The Midas
Touch Bet You Sell Your Soul Cuz Your
God Is Such You Don't Care You Kill For
The Money Do Or Dare The Thrill For
The Money

Are You Infected With The Same Disease
Of Lust, Gluttony And Greed? Then Watch
The Ones With The Biggest Smiles
The Idle Jabbers Cuz They're The Backstabbers

If You Know Its A Lie Then You Will Swear It
If You Give It With Guilt Then You Will Bear It
If Its Taking A Chance Then You Will Dare It

You Do Anything For Money...

(Chorus)

You Say You Wouldn't Do It For All The Money
In The World I Don't Think So If You Show Me
The Man Then I Will Sell Him If You Ask Me
To Lie Then I Will Tell Him If You're Stealing
With God Then You Will Hell Him

You Do Anything For Money

(Chorus)

Come Together

Here Come Ol' Flat Top
He Come Groovin' Up Slowly
He's Got Joo Joo Eyeball
He One Holy Roller
He Got Hair Down To His Knees
Got To Be A Joker He Just Do What
He Please

He Wear No Shoe Shine
He's Got Toe Jam Football
He's Got Monkey Finger
He Shoot Coca-Cola
He Say "I Know You, You Know Me"
One Thing I Can Tell You Is You
Got To Be Free

Come Together
Right Now
Over Me

He Bag Production
He's Got Walrus Gum-Boot
He's Got Ono Sideboard
He One Spinal Cracker
He Got Feet Down Through His Knees
Hold You In His Arm 'Til
You Can Feel His Disease

Come Together
Right Now
Over Me
Come Together Babe
Come Together Babe
Come Together
Come Together

He Roller Coaster
He's Got Early Warning
He's Got Muddy Water
He One Mojo Filter
He Say "One And One And One Is
Three" Got To Be Good Looking 'Cause
He's So Hard To See

Come Together
Right Now
Over Me

HIStory - Past, Present And Future - Book 1

You Are Not Alone

Another Day Has Gone
I'm Still All Alone
How Could This Be
You're Not Here With Me
You Never Said Goodbye
Someone Tell Me Why
Did You Have To Go
And Leave My World So Cold

Everyday I Sit And Ask Myself
How Did Love Slip Away
Something Whispers In My Ear
And Says That You Are Not Alone
For I Am Here With You
Though You're Far Away
I Am Here To Stay

But You Are Not Alone
For I Am Here With You
Though We're Far Apart
You're Always In My Heart
But You Are Not Alone

'Lone, 'Lone Why, 'Lone

Just The Other Night
I Thought I Heard You Cry
Asking Me To Come
And Hold You In My Arms
I Can Hear Your Prayers
Your Burdens I Will Bear
But First I Need Your Hand
Then Forever Can Begin

Everyday I Sit And Ask Myself
How Did Love Slip Away
Something Whispers In My Ear And
Says That You Are Not Alone
For I Am Here With You
Though You're Far Away
I Am Here To Stay

For You Are Not Alone
For I Am Here With You
Though We're Far Apart
You're Always In My Heart
For You Are Not Alone

Whisper Three Words And I'll
Come Runnin' And Girl You Know
That I'll Be There I'll Be There

You Are Not Alone
For I Am Here With You
Though You're Far Away
I Am Here To Stay
For You Are Not Alone
For I Am Here With You
Though We're Far Apart
You're Always In My Heart

For You Are Not Alone
For I Am Here With You
Though You're Far Away
I Am Here To Stay

For You Are Not Alone
For I Am Here With You
Though We're Far Apart
You're Always In My Heart

Childhood

Have You Seen My Childhood?
I'm Searching For The World That I Come From
'Cause I've Been Looking Around
In The Lost And Found Of My Heart...
No One Understands Me
They View It As Such Strange Eccentricities...
'Cause I Keep Kidding Around
Like A Child, But Pardon Me...

People Say I'm Not Okay
'Cause I Love Such Elementary Things...
It's Been My Fate To Compensate,
For The Childhood
I've Never Known...

Have You Seen My Childhood?
I'm Searching For That Wonder In My Youth
Like Pirates In Adventurous Dreams,
Of Conquest And Kings On The Throne...

Before You Judge Me, Try Hard To Love Me,
Look Within Your Heart Then Ask,
Have You Seen My Childhood?

People Say I'm Strange That Way
'Cause I Love Such Elementary Things,
It's Been My Fate To Compensate,
For The Childhood I've Never Known...

Have You Seen My Childhood?
I'm Searching For That Wonder In My Youth
Like Fantastical Stories To Share
The Dreams I Would Dare, Watch Me Fly...

Before You Judge Me, Try Hard To Love Me.
The Painful Youth I've Had

Have You Seen My Childhood...

Tabloid Junkies

Speculate To Break The One You Hate
Circulate The Lie You Confiscate
Assassinate And Mutilate
As The Hounding Media In Hysteria
Who's The Next For You To Resurrect
JFK Exposed The CIA
Truth Be Told The Grassy Knoll
As The Blackmail Story In All Your Glory

It's Slander
You Say It's Not A Sword
But With Your Pen You Torture Men
You'd Crucify The Lord
And You Don't Have To Read It, Read It
And You Don't Have To Eat It, Eat It
To Buy It Is To Feed It, Feed It
So Why Do We Keep Foolin' Ourselves

Just Because You Read It In A Magazine
Or See It On The TV Screen
Don't Make It Factual
Though Everybody Wants To Read All About
It Just Because You Read It In A Magazine
Or See It On The TV Screen
Don't Make It Factual, Actual
They Say He's Homosexual

Tabloid Junkies (cont)

In The Hood rame Him If You Could
Shoot To Kill To Blame Him If You Will
If He Dies Sympathize Such False Witnesses
Damn Self Righteousness In The Black
Stab Me In The Back In The Face To Lie
And Shame The Race Heroine And Marilyn
As The Headline Stories Of All Your Glory

It's Slander With The Words You Use
You're A Parasite In Black And White
Do Anything For News And You Don't
Go And Buy It, Buy It And They Won't
Glorify It, 'Fy It To Read It Sanctifies It,
Fies It Then Why Do We Keep Foolin'
Ourselves Just Because You Read It In A
Magazine Or See It On The TV Screen
Don't Make It Factual Everybody Wants
To Read All About It Just Because You
Read It In A Magazine Or See It On The
TV Screen Don't Make It Factual See,
But Everybody Wants To Believe All
About It

Just Because You Read It In A Magazine
Or See It On The TV Screen
Don't Make It Factual See, But Everybody
Wants To Believe All About It
Just Because You Read It In A Magazine
Or See It On The TV Screen
Don't Make It Factual, Actual
She's Blonde And She's Bisexual

Scandal With The Words You Use
You're A Parasite In Black And White
Do Anything For News
And You Don't Go And Buy It, Buy It
And They Won't Glorify It, 'Fy It
To Read It Sanctifies It, 'Fies It
Why Do We Keep Foolin' Ourselves
Slander
You Say It's Not A Sin
But With Your Pen You Torture Men
Then Why Do We Keep Foolin' Ourselves

Just Because You Read It In A Magazine
Or See It On The TV Screen
Don't Make It Factual
Though Everybody Wants To Read
All About It Just Because You Read It
In A Magazine Or See It On The TV
Screen Don't Make It Factual
See, But Everybody Wants To Read All
About It

Just Because You Read It In A Magazine
Or See It On The TV Screen
Don't Make It Factual
Just Because You Read It In A Magazine
Or See It On The TV Screen
Don't Make It Factual
Just Because You Read It In A Magazine
Or See It On The TV Screen
Don't Make It Factual, Actual
You're So Damn Disrespectable

HIStory - Past, Present And Future - Book 1

2 Bad

Told Me That You're Doin' Wrong
Word Out Shockin' All Alone
Cryin' Wolf Ain't Like A Man
Throwin' Rocks To Hide Your Hands
You Ain't Done Enough For Me
You Ain't Done Enough For Me
You Are Disgustin' Me, Yeah Yeah
You're Aiming Just For Me
You Are Disgustin' Me
Just Want Your Cut From Me
But Too Bad, Too Bad

Look Who Just Walked In The Place
Dead And Stuffy In The Face
Look Who's Standing If You Please
Though You Tried To Bring Me To My Knees

Too Bad Too Bad About It
Why Don't You Scream And Shout It
Too Bad Too Bad About It
Why Don't You Just Scream And Shout It
Too Bad Too Bad About It
Why Don't You Scream And Shout It
Too Bad Too Bad About It
Why Don't You Just Scream And Shout It

Hell All Up In Hollywood
Sayin' That You Got It Good
Creepin' From A Dusty Hole
Tales Of What Somebody Told
What Do You Want From Me?
What Do You Want From Me?
Tired Of You Haunting Me, Yeah Yeah
You're Aiming Just For Me
You Are Disgustin' Me
You Got Blood Lust For Me
But Too Bad, Too Bad

Look Who Got Slapped In The Face
It's Dead And Stuffy In The Place
I'm Right Back Where I Wanna Be
I'm Standin' Though You're Kickin' Me

(repeat)
[Rap: Shaquille O'Neal]
Life's About A Dream
I'm Really Undefeated When MJ Is On My
Team, Theme Reality Brings Forth Realizm

It's The Man Of Steel Organizm, Twizm
Not From The Prizm, Take Charge Like
Manilla Nine Five Shaq Represent With
The Thrilla Grab My Crotch, Twist My
Knee, Then I'm Through Mike's Bad, I'm
Bad Who Are You

(repeat)

HIStory

He Got Kicked In The Back
He Say That He Needed That
He Hot Willed In The Face
Keep Daring To Motivate
He Say One Day You Will See
His Place In World History
He Dares To Be Recognized
The Fires Deep In His Eyes

How Many Victims Must There Be
Slaughtered In Vain Across The Land
And How Many Struggles Must There
Be Before We Choose To Live The
Prophet's Plan Everybody Sing

Every Day Create Your History
Every Path You Take You're Leaving
Your Legacy Every Soldier Dies In His
Glory Every Legend Tells Of Conquest
And Liberty

Don't Let No One Get You Down
Keep Movin' On Higher Ground
Keep Flying Until
You Are The King Of The Hill
No Force Of Nature Can Break
Your Will To Self Motivate
She Say This Face That You See
Is Destined For History

How Many People Have To Cry
The Song Of Pain And Grief Across
The Land And How Many Children
Have To Die Before We Stand To Lend
A Healing Hand Everybody Sing

Every Day Create Your History
Every Path You Take You're Leaving
Your Legacy Every Soldier Dies In His
Glory Every Legend Tells Of Conquest
And Liberty Every Day Create Your History
Every Page You Turn You're Writing Your
Legacy Every Hero Dreams Of Chivalry
Every Child Should Sing Together In Harmony

All Nations Sing
Let's Harmonize All Around The World

How Many Victims Must There Be
Slaughtered In Vain Across The Land
And How Many Children Must We See
Before We Learn To Live As Brothers
And Leave One Family Oh

Every Day Create Your History
Every Path You Take You're Leaving Your Legacy
Every Soldier Dies In His Glory
Every Legend Tells Of Conquest And Liberty
Every Day Create Your History
Every Page You Turn You're Writing Your Legacy
Every Hero Dreams Of Chivalry
Every Child Should Sing Together In Harmony

A Soldier Dies A Mother Cries
The Promised Child Shines In A Baby's Eyes
All Nations Sing
Let's Harmonize All Around The World

Little Susie

Somebody Killed Little Susie
The Girl With The Tune
Who Sings In The Daytime At Noon
She Was There Screaming
Beating Her Voice In Her Doom
But Nobody Came To Her Soon...

A Fall Down The Stairs
Her Dress Torn
Oh The Blood In Her Hair...
A Mystery So Sullen In Air
She Lie There So Tenderly
Fashioned So Slenderly
Lift Her With Care,
With The Blood In Her Hair

Everyone Came To See
The Girl That Now Is Dead
So Blind Stare The Eyes In Her Head...
And Suddenly A Voice From The Crowd Said
This Girl Lived In Vain
Her Face Bear Such Agony, Such Strain

But Only The Man From Next Door
Knew Little Susie And How He Cried
As He Reached Down
To Close Susie's Eyes...
She Lie There So Tenderly
Fashioned So Slenderly
Lift Her With Care
With The Blood In Her Hair...

It Was All For God's Sake
For Her Singing The Tune
For Someone To Feel Her Despair
To Be Damned To Know Hoping
Is Dead And You're Doomed
Then To Scream Out
And Nobody's There

She Knew No One Cared

Father Left Home, Poor Mother Died
Leaving Susie Alone
Grandfather's Soul Too Had Flown
No One To Care
Just To Love Her
How Much Can One Bear
Rejecting The Needs In Her Prayers

Neglection Can Kill
Like A Knife In Your Soul
Oh It Will
Little Susie Fought So Hard To Live...
She Lie There So Tenderly
Fashioned So Slenderly
Lift Her With Care
So Young And So Fair

SMILE

Smile, Though Your Heart Is Aching
Smile, Even Though It's Breaking
When There Are Clouds In The Sky
You'll Get By...

If You Smile
With Your Fear And Sorrow
Smile And Maybe Tomorrow
You'll Find That Life Is Still Worthwhile
If You Just

Light Up Your Face With Gladness
Hide Every Trace Of Sadness
Although A Tear May Be Ever So Near
That's The Time You Must Keep On Trying
Smile, What's The Use Of Crying
You'll Find That Life Is Still Worthwhile
If You Just

Smile, Though Your Heart Is Aching
Smile, Even Though It's Breaking
When There Are Clouds In The Sky
You'll Get By...

If You Smile
Through Your Fear And Sorrow
Smile And Maybe Tomorrow
You'll Find That Life Is Still Worthwhile
If You Just Smile

That's The Time You Must Keep On Trying
Smile, What's The Use Of Crying
You'll Find That Life Is Still Worthwhile
If You Just Smile

BLOOD ON THE DANCE FLOOR - HIStory In Mix

Blood On The Dance Floor

She Got Your Number She Know Your Game
She Put You Under It's So Insane

Since You Seduced Her How Does It Feel
To Know That Woman Is Out To Kill

Every Night Stance Is Like Takin' A Chance
It's Not About Love And Romance
And Now You're Gonna Get It

Every Hot Man Is Out Takin' A Chance
It's Not About Love And Romance
And Now You Do Regret It

To Escape The World I've Got To Enjoy
That Simple Dance And It Seemed That
Everything Was On My Side She Seemed
Sincere Like It Was Love And True Romance
And Now She's Out To Get Me And I Just
Can't Take It Just Can't Break It

Susie Got Your Number And Susie Ain't
Your Friend Look Who Took You Under
With Seven Inches In Blood Is On The
Dance Floor Blood Is On The Knife
Susie's Got Your Number And Susie Says
Its Right

She Got Your Number How Does It Feel
To Know This Stranger Is Out To Kill
She Got Your Baby It Happened Fast
If You Could Only Erase The Past

Every Night Stance Is Like Takin A Chances
It's Not About Love And Romance
And Now You're Gonna Get It

Every Hot Man Is Out Takin' A Chance
It's Not About Love And Romance
And Now You Do Regret It

To Escape The World I Got To Enjoy This
Simple Dance And It Seemed That
Everything Was On My Side It Seemed
Sincere Like It Was Love And True Romance
And Now She's Out To Get Me And I Just
Can't Take It Just Can't Break It

Susie Got Your Number And Susie Ain't
Your Friend Look Who Took You Under
With Seven Inches In Blood Is On The
Dance Floor Blood Is On The Knife
Susie Got Your Number You Know
Susie Says Its Right

Susie's Got Your Number Susie Ain't
Your Friend Look Who Took You Under
She Put Seven Inches In Blood Is On
The Dance Floor Blood Is On The Knife
Susie's Got Your Number Susie
Says Its Right

It Was Blood On The Dance Floor
It Was Blood On The Dance Floor
It Was Blood On The Dance Floor
It Was Blood On The Dance Floor

And I Just Can't Take It The Girl
Won't Break It Ooo

Demerol

He Got Flat Baby Kick In The Back Baby
A Heart Attack Baby I Need Your Body
A Hot Kiss Honey He's Just A Bitch Baby
You Make Me Sick Baby So Unrelying
I'm Such A Swine Baby All Down The
Line Daddy I Hate Your Kind Baby
So Unreliable

A Hot Buzz Baby He's One Of Us Baby
Another Drug Baby You So Desire
Trust In Me Trust In Me Put All Your
Trust In Me You're Doin' Morphine Hoo!

They Got Place Baby Kicked In The Face
Baby You Hate Your Race Baby You're
Just A Liar

Your Every Lick Baby Your Dog's A Bitch
Baby You Make Me Sick Baby You Sole
Survivor She Never Cut From Me
She Never Cut Baby I Had To Work
Baby You Just A Rival

Always To Please Daddy Right Up And
Leave Daddy You're Throwing Shame
Daddy So Undesirable

Trust In Me Just In Me Put All Your
Trust In Me You're Doin' Morphine

Go'on Babe

Relax This Won't Hurt You Before I
Put It In Close Your Eyes And Count
To Ten Don't Cry I Won't Convert You
There's No Need To Dismay
Close Your Eyes And Drift Away

Demerol Demerol Oh God He's Taking
Demerol Demerol Demerol Oh God
He's Taking Demerol

He's Tried Hard To Convince Her
To Be Over What He Had Today
He Wants It Twice As Bad Don't Cry
I Won't Resent You Yesterday You Had
His Trust Today He's Taking Twice
As Much

Demerol Demerol Oh God He's Taking
Demerol Hee-Hee-Hee Demerol
Demerol Oh My Oh God It's Demerol
Hee Oooh Oh!

He Got Shit Baby Your Dog's A Bitch Baby
You Make Me Sick Baby You Are A Liar

Is Truth A Game Daddy To Win The Fame
Baby It's All The Same Baby You're So
Reliable

Trust In Me Trust In Me Put All Your
Trust In Me She's Doin' Morphine Hoo!

You Just Sit Around Just Talkin' Nothing
You're Takin' Morphine Hoo! Go'on Baby
You Just Sit Around Just Talking About It
You're Takin' Morphine Hoo-Hoo!
Just Sit Around Just Talking Nothing About It
You're Takin' Morphine You Just Sit Around
Just Talking About It You're Taking Morphine
You Just Sit Around Just Talkin' Nothin'
And Takin' Morphine

Hoo-Hoo I'm Going Down Baby
You're Talkin' Morphine

Go'on Baby! Hoo! Hoo! Morphine!
Do It! Hoo! He's Takin' Morphine

Superfly Sister

Love Ain't What It Used To Be
That Is What They're Tellin' Me
Push It In Stick It Out
That Ain't What It's All About

He Wanna Do Something Keen To You
He Wanna Wrap His Arms All Around
You Girl He Wanna Shake It Up Shake
It Down Doing It Right He Wanna Jump
Back Half Flap Doing It Right He Wanna
Lay You Down Turn It Up Kicking It Loose
He Wanna Fly High Nigh High Baby For
You'se He Wanna Motormouth Float
Around Baby The Back He Wanna Shake
It Up Shake It Down Moving Round Ha Ha

Love Ain't What It Used To Be
That Is What They're Tellin' Me
Push It In Stick It Out
That Ain't What It's All About

Susie Like To Agitate
Get The Boy And Make Him Wait
Mother's Preaching Abraham
Brothers They Don't Give A Damn
He Wanna Do Something Keen To You
He Wanna Wrap His Arms All Around
You Girl He Wanna Do It Up Keep It
High Deep In The Night He Wanna
Eye Ball Get Hard Playing It Right
He Wanna Turn The Key Hurt The Sheets
Move To The Left He Wanna Hot Scrub
Hot Love Making It Wet He Wanna Give
Hot Jump Shot Move To The Left He
Wanna Time Bar Slam Dunk

Love Ain't What It Used To Be
That Is What They're Tellin' Me

Push It In Stick It Out
That Ain't What It's All About
Sister Say She Love Him Some
God Is Jammin' On The Run
Mother's Preaching Abraham
Brothers They Don't Give A Damn
Johnny's Begging Pretty Please
Keep The Brother On His Knees
Susie Likes To Agitate
Get The Boy And Make Him Wait

Sister's Marries To A Hood
Sayin' That She Got It Good
Holy Mary Mercy Me
I Can't Believe The Things I See

Thinkin' That They Got It Made
They Doin' What They Used To Hate
Push It In Stick It Out That Ain't
What It's All About That Ain't What
It's All About Holy Mary Mercy Me
I Can't Believe The Things I See
Mother's Preaching Abraham Brothers
They Don't Give A Damn Sister Say
She Loves Him Some God Is Jammin'
All Around Holy Mary Mercy Me
I Can't Believe The Things I See

You're Doin' It You're DirtyKeep
Doin' It You're Dirty Keep Nasty You're
Nasty You're Doin' It You're Dirty
You're Dirty You're Doin' It You're
Nasty You're Doin' It Keep Dirty Keep
Dirty You Really Want It Oooh!

Holy Mary Mercy Me

I Can't Believe The Things I See
Push It In Stick It Out
That Ain't What It's All About

BLOOD ON THE DANCE FLOOR - HIStory in Mix

Ghost

There's A Ghost Down In The Hall
There's A Ghoul Upon The Bed
There's Something In The Walls
There's Blood Up On The Stairs
And It's Floating Through The Room
And There's Nothing I Can See
And I Know That That's The Truth
Because Now It's Onto Me

I Don't Understand It Hey
I Don't Understand It! Aaow

There's A Tappin' In The Floor
There's A Creak Behind The Door
There's A Rocking In The Chair
But There's No-One Sitting There
There's A Ghostly Smell Around
But Nobody To Be Found
And A Coughin' And A Yawnin'
Where A Restless Soul Is Going

Don't Understand It Hey!
Don't Understand It Hey

And Who Gave You The Right To
Shake My Family? And Who Gave
You The Right To Shake My Baby,
She Needs Me And Who Gave You
The Right To Shake My Family Tree?
You Put A Knife In My Back
Shot An Arrow In Me!
Tell Me Are You The Ghost Of Jealousy
The Ghost Of Jealousy

There's A Tappin In The Floor
There's A Creak Behind The Door
There's A Rocking In The Chair
But Nobody's Sitting There
There's A Ghostly Smell Around
But Nobody To Be Found
And A Coughin' And A Yawnin'
Where A Restless Soul Is Going

Don't Understand It! Yeah Yeah!
Don't Understand It! Your Just A
Dog Gone! Aaow!

And Who Gave You The Right To
Scare My Family? And Who Gave
You The Right To Scare My Baby,
She Needs Me And Who Gave You
The Right To Shake My Family Tree?
And Who Gave You The Right To
Take Intrusion, To See Me? And Who
Gave You The Right To Shake My Family?
And Who Gave You The Right To Hurt
My Baby, She Needs Me And Who Gave
You The Right To Shake My Family Tree?
You Put A Knife In My Back, Shot An
Arrow In Me! Tell Me Are You The Ghost
Of Jealousy A Suckin' Ghost Of Jealousy
Aaow!

Ghost (cont)

And Who Gave You The Right To Shake
My Family? And Who Gave You The Right
To Shake My Baby, She Needs Me And
Who Gave You The Right To Shake My
Family Tree? And Who Gave You The Right
To Take, Intrusion To See Me? And Who
Gave You The Right To Hurt My Family?
And Who Gave You The Right Hurt My Baby,
She Needs Me And Who Gave You The Right
To Shake My Family Tree? You Put A Knife
In My Back Shot An Arrow In Me! Tell Me
Are You The Ghost Of Jealousy
The Ghost Of Jealousy

Aaow Dog Gone
But There's No Doubt About It, Piece Of Mind
Tell Me Are You The Ghost Of Jealousy

Is It Scary

There's A Ghost Out In The Hall
Theirs A Goul Beneath The Bed
Now It's Coming Through The Walls
Now It's Coming Down The Stairs

Then There's Screaming In The Dark
Hear The Beating Of His Heart
Can You Feel It In The Air
Ghosts Be Hiding Everywhere

I'm Gonna Be
Exactly What You Wanna See
It's You Whose Haunting Me
Your Warning Me
To Be The Stranger
In Your Life

Am I Amusing You
Or Just Confusing You
Am I The Beast
You Visualized
And If You Wanna To See
Eccentricalities
I'll Be Grotesque
Before Your Eyes

Let Them All Materialize

Is That Scary For You Baby
Am I Scary For You Oh
Is It Scary For You Baby
Is It Scary For You

You Know The Stranger Is You
Is It Scary For You Baby
There's A Creak Beneath The Floor
There's A Creak Behind The Door
There's A Rocking In The Chair
But Nobody Sitting There
There's A Ghostly Smell Around
But Nobody To Be Found
And A Coughin' And A Yawnin'
Where Restless Soul's Spoke

Is It Scary (cont)

I'm Gonna Be
Exactly What You Gonna See
So Did You Come To Me
To See Your Fantasies
Performed Before Your Very Eyes

A Haunting Ghostly Treat
The Foolish Trickery
And Spirits Dancing
In The Light

But If You Came To See
The Truth The Purity
It's Here Inside
A Lonely Heart

So Let The Performance Start

Is That Scary For You Baby
Am I Scary For You Oh
Am I Scary For You Baby
Am I Scary For You
So Tell Me Is It Scary For You Baby
So Tell Me Is It Crazy For You Baby
Am I Scary For You

You Know The Stranger Is You
Am I Scary For Ya

Masquerade The Heart
Is The Height Of Haunting Souls
Just Not What You Seek Of Me
Can The Heart Reveal The Proof
Like A Mirror Reveals The Truth
See The Evil One Is You

Is That Scary For You Baby
Am I Scary For You Oh
Am I Scary For You Baby
Is It Scary For You
So Tell Me Am I Scary For You Baby
Am I Scary For Ya Baby
Is Is Scary For Ya Baby
Am I Scary For You
(I Don't Wanna Talk About It)

Am I Scary For You Baby
Am I Scary For You
I'm Tired Of Being Abused
You Know You're Scaring Me Too
I See The Evil Is You
Is It Scary For You Baby

INVINCIBLE

Unbreakable

Now I'm Just Wondering Why You Think
That You Can Get To Me With Anything
Seems Like You'd Know By Now
When And How I Get Down
And With All That I've Been Through,
I'm Still Around

Don't You Ever Make No Mistake
Baby I've Got What It Takes
And There's No Way You'll Ever Get To Me
Why Can't You See That You'll Never Ever
Hurt Me 'Cause I Won't Let It Be, See I'm
Too Much For You Baby

(Chorus)
You Can't Believe It, You Can't Conceive It
And You Can't Touch Me, 'Cause I'm
Untouchable And I Know You Hate It, And
You Can't Take It You'll Never Break Me,
'Cause I'm Unbreakable

Now You Can't Stop Me Even Thought
You Think That If You Block Me, You've
Done Your Thing And When You Bury
Me Underneath All Your Pain
I´M Steady Laughin', While Surfacing

Don't You Ever Make No Mistake
Baby I've Got What It Takes
And There's No Way You'll Ever Get To
Me Why Can't You See That You'll Never
Ever Hurt Me 'Cause I Won't Let It Be,
See I'm Too Much For You Baby

(Chorus 2x)

You Can Try To Stop Me, But It Won't
Do A Thing No Matter What You Do,
I'm Still Gonna Be Here Through All Your
Lies And Silly Games I'm A Still Remain
The Same, I'm Unbreakable

(Notorious B.I.G.)
Uh, Uh, What, Uh A Lime To A Lemon,
My D.C. Women Bringin In Ten G
Minimums To Condos With Elevators In 'Em
Vehicles With Televisions In 'Em
Watch They Entourage Turn Yours To Just
Mirages Disappearing Acts, Strictly Nines
And Macs Killers Be Serial, Copperfield
Material My Dreams Is Vivid, Work Hard
To Live It Any Place I Visit, I Got Land There
How Can Players Stand There And Say I
Sound Like ThemHELLO?! Push Wigs Back
And Push Six Coupes That's Yellow Plus
Clips That Expand From Hand To Elbow
Spray Up Your Day's Inn, Any 'Telle You In
Crack Braggin Sick Of Braggin How My
Mink Be Draggin Desert Ease Street Sweeper
Inside The Beamer Wagon I Rely On Bed-
Stuy To Shut It Down If I Die Put That
On My Diamond Bezel, You're Messin
With The Devil WHAT.!!

(Chorus x3)

Heartbreaker

Deceitful Eyes, She's Got Those
Come Get Me Thighs She Only
Knows How Low That She Can Go
She Speaks The Lines That Can
Control My Mind Wherever She
Goes I Know My Eyes Follow She
Blew A Kiss, I Swear That It Was
Meant Only For Me, Then Spoke
With Her Body Her Only Goal Is
Just To Take Control And I Can't
Believe That I Can´T Tell Her No

(Chorus)
That Girl I Can't Take Her
Should Have Known She Was A
Heartbreaker That Girl I Can't
Take Her Should Have Seen Right
Through Her She's A Heartbreaker
That Girl I Can't Take Her Should
Have Seen It Coming Heartbreaker
That Girl I Can't Take Her
Should Have Seen Right Thriough
Her She's A Heartbreaker

She Plays A Game With Such An
Innocent Face I Didn't Know
Heartbreaking Was Her Case Her
Actions Confess And Put Me
Through The Test I Was Surprised
That I Was Caught Inside Now She's
Thinking That I Will Never Know
Ans She'll Keep Playing Until I
Let Her Go But I Hope In Time
That She Will Finally Realize
I'm Onto Her Game And She'll
Get Played The Same

(Chours x2)

I Never Thought That I Would Stop
Dreamin' About You Stop Being
Without You But Everyone Told
Me So, To Stop Caring About You
And Start Being Without You But
I'll Find A Way To Go And Start
Doin' Without You And Stop
Talkin' Aboout You And What
Will She Say? She Will Say I Was
The Man That Got Away

[Rap]

That Girl I Can't Take Her
Should Have Known She Was A
Heartbreaker That Girl I Can't
Take Her Should Have Seen Right
Through Her She's A Heartbreaker
That Girl I Can't Take Her Should
Have Seen It Coming Heartbreaker
That Girl I Can't Take Her
Should Have Seen Right Thriough
Her She's A Heartbreaker

Invincible

If I Could Tear Down These Walls That
Keep You And I Apart I Know I Could
Claim Your Heart And Our Perfect Love
Will Start But Girl You Just Won't
Approve Of The Things That I Do When
All I Do Is For You But Still You Say It
Ain't Cool

If There's Somebody Else, He Can't Love
You Like Me And He Says He'll Treat You
Well, He Can't Treat You Like Me And
He's Buying Diamonds And Pearls, He
Can't Do It Like Me And He's Taking
You All Across The World, He Can't
Trick You Like Me

So Why Ain't You Feelin' Me, She's
Invincible But I Can Do Anything,
She's Invincible Even When I Beg
And Plead, She's Invincible Girl Won't
Give In To Me, She's Invincible

Well, Well, See Well, Well Come Now
How Many Times I've Told You Of
All The Things I Would Do But I
Cant Seem To Get Through No
Matter How I Try To So Tell Me
How Does It Seem That You Ain't
Checking For Me When I Know That
I Could Be More Than You Could
Ever Dream

If There's Somebody Else, He Can't Love
You Like Me And He Says He'll Treat You
Well, He Can't Treat You Like Me And
He's Buying Diamonds And Pearls, He
Can't Do It Like Me And He's Talking
You All Across The World, He Can't
Trick You Like Me

Why Ain't You Feelin' Me, She's
Invincible But I Can Do Anything,
She's Invincible Even When I Beg
And Plead, She's Invincible Girl Won't
Give In To Me, She's Invincible

Some Way I'll Have To Prove All
That I Said I Would Do Giving You
Everything, Fulfilling Your Fantasy
Then Maybe You'll Change Your Mind
And Finally Give In Time Then I'll Be
Showing You What Other Men Are
Supposed To Do For You My Baby

[Rap]

Why Ain't You Feelin' Me, She's
Invincible But I Can Do Anything,
She's Invincible Even When I Beg
And Plead, She's Invincible Girl Won't
Give In To Me, She's Invincible

INVINCIBLE

Break Of Dawn

Hold My Hand, Feel The Touch Of
Your Body Cling To Mine You And Me,
Makin' Love All The Way Through
Another Night I Remember You And I
Walking Though The Park At Night
Kiss And Touch, Nothing Much, Let It
Blow Just Touch And Go

Love Me More, Never Leave Me Alone
By House Of Love People Talk, People
Say What We Have Is Just A Game
Oh, I'll Never Let You Go, Come Here
Girl Just Got To Make Sweet Love 'Til
The Break Of Dawn

(Chorus)

I Don't Want The Sun To Shine I Wanna
Make Love Just This Magic In Your Eyes
And In My Heart I Don't Know What
I'm Gonna Do I Can't Stop Lovin' You
I Won't Stop 'Til Break Of Dawn Makin'
Love

Hold My Hand, Feel The Sweat, Yes
You've Got Me Nervous Yet Let Me
Groove, Let Me Soothe, Let Me Take
You On A Cruise There's Imagination
I Bet You've Never Been There Before
Have You Ever Wanted To Dream About
Those Places You've Never Know

Break Of Dawn, There's No Sun Up In
The Sky Break Of Dawn, I Can See It
In Your Eyes Break Of Dawn, Girl You
Got To Understand It's The Way That
I Love You, Let Me Show You I'm Your
Man Break Of Dawn

[Chorus X 2]

Let's Not Wait, The Sun Is Out, Let's
Get Up And Let's Get Out It's The Day,
A Brand New Day, Let's Both Go Outside
And Play Let Us Walk Down The Park,
Makin' Love 'Til It's Dark Let Me Move,
Let Me Soothe, 'Til The Break Of Dawn
And You Know It's True, Oh

[Chorus X 3]

Heaven Can Wait

(Chorus)

Tell The Angels No, I Don't Wanna Leave
My Baby Alone I Don't Want Nobody
Else To Hold You That's A Chance I'll Take
Baby I'll Stay, Heaven Can Wait
No, If The Angels Took Me From This Earth
I Would Tell Them Bring Me Back To Her
It's A Chance I'll Take, Maybe I'll Stay Heaven
Can Wait

You're Beautiful
Each Moment Spent With You Is Simply
Wonderful This Love I Have For You Girl
It's Incredible And I Don't Know What
I'd Do, If I Can't Be With You The World
Could Not Go On So Every Night I Pray
If The Lord Should Come For Me Before
I Wake I Wouldn't Wanna Go If I Can't
See Your Face, Can't Hold You Close
What Good Would Heaven Be If The
Angels Came For Me I'd Tell Them No

(Chorus)

Unthinkable Me Sitting Up In The Clouds
And You Are All Alone The Time Might
Come Around When You'd Be Moving On
I'd Turn It All Around And Try To Get Back
Down To My Baby Girl Can't Stand To See
Nobody Kissing, Touching Her Couldn't
Take Nobody Loving You The Way We Were
What Good Would Heaven Be If The Angels
Come For Me I'd Tell Them No

(Chorus)

Oh No, Can't Be Without My Baby
Won't Go, Without Her I'd Go Crazy
Oh No, Guess Heaven Will Be Waiting
Ooh Oh No, Can't Be Without My Baby
Won't Go, Without Her I'd Go Crazy
Oh No, Guess Heaven Will Be Waiting
Ooh

(Chorus)

Just Leave Us Alone, Leave Us Alone
Please Leave Us Alone

You Rock My World

My Life Will Never Be The Same
Cause Girl You Came And Changed
The Way I Walk, The Way I Talk
I Cannot Explain These Things I Feel
For You But Girl You Know It's True
Stay With Me, Fulfill My Dreams
And I'll Be All You Need Ooh It
Feels So Right, Girl I've Searched For
The Perfect Love All My Life
All My Life Ooh Feels Like I Have
Finally Found A Perfect Love This Time
I Have Finally Found, Come On Girl

You Rocked My World, You Know You
Did And Everything I Own I Give
The Rarest Love, Who'd Think I'd Find
Someone Like You To Call Mine
You Rocked My World, You Know You
Did And Everything I Own I Give
The Rarest Love, Who'd Think I'd Find
Someone Like You To Call Mine

In Time, I Knew That Love Would Bring
Such Happiness To Me I Tried To Keep
My Sanity I've Waited Patiently And Girl
You Know It Seems My Life Is So Complete
A Love That's True, Because Of You
Keep Doing What You Do Ooh Think
That I (Girl) Finally Find The Perfect
Love I Search For All My Life Search For
All My Life Ooh Who'd Think I'd Find
Such A Perfect Love That's Awesomely
So Right Oooh, Girl

(Chorus 2x)

And Girl, I Know That This Is Love
I Feel The Magic All In The Air
And Girl, I'll Never Get Enough
That's Why I Always Have To Have
You Here Hooh!

(Chorus 2x)

You Rock My World! (You Rocked My
World, You Know You Did) The Way
You Talk To Me, The Way You Lovin' Me
The Way You.. You Give It To Me!
(You Rocked My World, You Know
You Did) Yeah, Yeah Yeaaah! Yeaaah!
(You Rocked My World, You Know
You Did) You Rock My World, You
Rock My World! You Rock My World
(Give It To Me) Come On Girl

You Rocked My World, You Know You
Did (Come On Girl!) And Everything I
Own I Give (Baby Baby Baby) The Rarest
Love, Who'd Think I'd Findv (Its You
And Me!) Someone Like You To Call
Mine (Its You Me!) You Rocked My
World, You Know You Did
And Everything I Own I Give
The Rarest Love, Who'd Think I'd Find
Someone Like You To Call Mine

INVINCIBLE

Butterflies

All You Gotta Do Is Just Walk Away
And Pass Me By Don't Acknowledge
My Smile When I Try To Say Hello
To You, Yeah And All You Gotta Do
Is Not Answer My Calls When I'm
Trying To Get Through To Keep
Me Wondering Why, When All I
Can Do Is Sigh I Just Wanna
Touch You

I Just Wanna Touch And Kiss
And I Wish That I Could Be With
You Tonight You Give Me Butterflies
Inside, Inside And I

All I Gotta Say Is That I Must Be
Dreaming, Can't Be Real You're
Not Here With Me, Still I Can Feel
You Near Me I Caress You, Let You
Taste Us, Just So Blissful Listen
I Would Give You Anything Baby,
Just Make My Dreams Come True
Oh Baby You Give Me Butterflies

I Just Wanna Touch And Kiss
And I Wish That I Could Be With
You Tonight You Give Me Butterflies
Inside, Inside And I I Just Wanna
Touch And Kiss And I Wish That I
Could Be With You Tonight You
Give Me Butterflies
Inside, Inside And I

If You Would Take My Hand, Baby
I Would Show You Guide You To
The Light Babe If You Would Be
My Love, Baby I Will Love You,
Love You 'Til The End Of Time

I Just Wanna Touch And Kiss
And I Wish That I Could Be With
You Tonight You Give Me Butterflies
Inside, Inside And I I Just Wanna
Touch And Kiss And I Wish That I
Could Be With You Tonight You
Give Me Butterflies Inside, Inside
And I I Just Wanna Touch And Kiss
And I Wish That I Could Be With
You Tonight You Give Me Butterflies
Inside, Inside And I

Speechless

Your Love Is Magical, That's How I Feel
But I Have Not The Words Here To Explain
Gone Is The Grace For Expressions Of Passion
But There Are Worlds And Worlds Of Ways To
Explain To Tell You How I Feel

But I Am Speechless, Speechless That's How
You Make Me Feel Though I'm With You
I Am Far Away And Nothing Is For Real
When I'm With You I Am Lost For Words,
I Don't Know What To Say My Head's
Spinning Like A Carousel, So Silently I Pray

Helpless And Hopeless, That's How I Feel
Inside Nothing's Real, But All Is Possible
If God Is On My Side When I'm With
You I Am In The Light Where I Cannot

Speechless (cont)

Speechless, Speechless, That's How You
Make Me Feel Though I'm With You I
Am Far Away And Nothing Is For Real
I'll Go Anywhere And Do Anything Just
To Touch Your Face There's No
Mountain High I Cannot Climb
I'm Humbled In Your Grace

Speechless, Speechless, That's How You
Make Me Feel Though I'm With You I
Am Lost For Words And Nothing Is
For Real Speechless, Speechless, That's
How You Make Me Feel Though I'm
With You I Am Far Away, And Nothing
Is For Real Speechless, Speechless, That's
How You Make Me Feel Though I'm With
You I Am Lost For Words And Nothing
Is For Real

Speechless

Your Love Is Magical, That's How I Feel
But In Your Presence I Am Lost For Words
Words Like, "I Love You."

2000 Watts

You May Now Apply, (You May Now Apply)
Your 3D Glasses (Your 3D Glasses)
As We Proceed (Prepare For Proceed)
2000 Watts (Repeated) Bass Note, Treble
Stereo Control How Low, You Go
Just Enough To Make Your Juices Flow
Press Play, Don't Stop Rotate, Too Hot
You Feel I'm Real I'm Everything You
Need, So Tell Me What's The Deal

(Chorus)

2000 Watts, 8 Ohms 200 Volts, Real Strong
Too Much Of That, Fuse Blown Be Careful
What You Say, Don't Overload 2000 Watts,
8 Ohms 200 Volts, Real Strong Too Much
Of That, Fuse Blown Be Careful What You
Say, Don't Overload

3D, High Speed Feedback, Dolby
Release Two Or Three When I Reach I
Can Go 'Til I Hit My Peak Compact Steelo
Chico, D-Lo Highpost Lady
Shorty Really Wanna Be There For Me

(Chorus X 2)

Yeah All Right Now. Are You Ready
Arhhh!... Watt... Dolby... Watt...
Baby, Baby, Don't

3 Dimensional High Speed Baby 3D
3D, 3D, 3D, Now Compact
Steelo Sing Low D-Low
High Post
Come On, Come On, Come On

(Chorus X 2)

Dance
Don't You Overload
Baby

You Are My Life

Once All Alone
I Was Lost In A World Of Strangers
No One To Trust
On My Own, I Was Lonely
You Suddenly Appeared
It Was Cloudy Before But Now It's All
Clear You Took Away The Fear
You Brought Me Back To Life

(Chorus)
You Are The Sun
You Make Me Shine
More Like The Stars
That Twinkle At Night
You Are The Moon
That Glows In My Heart
You're My Daytime My Nighttime
My World You Are My Life

Now I Wake Up Everyday
With This Smile Upon My Face
No More Tears, No More Pain
'Cause You Love Me
You Help Me Understand
That Love Is The Answer To All That I
Am And I'm A Better Man You Taught
Me By Sharing Your Life

You Are The Sun
You Make Me Shine
More Like The Stars
That Twinkle At Night
You Are The Moon
That Glows In My Heart
You're My Daytime My Nighttime
My World

You Are The Sun
You Make Me Shine
More Like The Stars
That Twinkle At Night
You Are The Moon
That Glows In My Heart
You're My Daytime My Nighttime
My World

You Gave Me Strength
When I Wasn't Strong
You Gave Me Hope When All Hope Is
Lost You Opened My Eyes When I
Couldn't See Love Was Always Here
Waiting For Me

You Are The Sun
You Make Me Shine
More Like The Stars
That Twinkle At Night
You Are The Moon
That Glows In My Heart
You're My Daytime My Nighttime
My World

(Chorus x2)

INVINCIBLE

Don't Walk Away

Don't Walk Away See I Just Can't
Find The Right Thing To Say
I Tried But All My Pain Gets In
The Way Tell Me What I Have
To Do So You'll Stay Should I
Get Down On My Knees And Pray
How Can I Stop Losing You How
Can I Begin To Say When There's
Nothing Left To Do But Walk Away

I Close My Eyes Just To Try And
See You Smile One More Time
But It's Been So Long Now All
I Do Is Cry Can't We Find Some
Love To Take This Away 'Cause
The Pain Gets Stronger Every Day
How Can I Begin Again How Am
I To Understand When There's
Nothing Left To Do But Walk Away

See Now Why All My Dreams Been
Broken I Don't Know Where We're
Going When Everything We Said
And All We Done Now Don't Let
Go, I Don't Wanna Walk Away

Why All My Dreams Been Broken
Don't Know Where We're Going
Everything Begins To Set Us Free
Can't You See, I Don't Wanna Walk Away

If You Go, I Won't Forget You Girl
Please Don't Go
Can't You See That You Will Always Be
You will always be
Even Though I Had To Let You Go
Don't You Leave Me, Don't You Leave Me
There' Nothing Left To Do
Don't Walk Away
If you go, I won't forget you girl
Can't you see that you will always be
Even though I had to let you go
There' nothing left to do
Don't walk away

Privacy

Ain't The Pictures Enough, Why Do
You Go Through So Much To Get
The Stories You Need, So You Can
Bury Me You've Got The People
Confused, You Tell The Stories You
Choose You Try To Get Me To Lose
The Man I Really Am

You Keep On Stalking Me, Invading
My Privacy Won't You Just Let Me Be
'Cause You Cameras Can't Control,
The Minds Of Those Who Know
That You'll Even Sell Your Soul
Just To Get A Story Sold

I Need My Privacy, I Need My Privacy
So Paparazzi, Get Away From Me Just
Get Away From Me

Some Of You Still Wonder Why, One Of
My Friends Had To Die To Get A Message
Across, That Yet You Haven't Heard My
Friend Was Chased And Confused, Like
Many Others I Knew But On That Cold
Winter Night, My Pride Was Snatched Away

She Get No Second Chance, She Just
Ridiculed And Harassed Please Tell My Why
Now There's A Lesson To Learn, Respect's
Not Given, It's Earned Stop Maliciously
Attacking My Integrity

I Need My Privacy, I Need My Privacy
So Paparazzi, Just Get Away From Me Just
Get Away From Me

Slash!

Now There's A Lesson To Learn, Stories Are
Twisted And Turned Stop Maliciously
Attacking My Integrity

I Need My Privacy, I Need My Privacy
So Paparazzi, Get Away From Me I Need
My Privacy, I Need My Privacy
So Paparazzi, Get Away From Me Privacy
Privacy, Privacy...

Cry

Somebody Shakes When The
Wind Blows Somebody's Missing
A Friend, Hold On Somebody's
Lacking A Hero And They Have
Not A Clue When It's All Gonna End

Stories Buried And Untold
Someone Is Hiding The Truth, Hold On
When Will This Mystery Unfold
And Will The Sun Ever Shine
In The Blind Man's Eyes When He Cries?

You Can Change The World (I Can't Do
It By Myself) You Can Touch The Sky
(Gonna Take Somebody's Help) You're
The Chosen One (I'm Gonna Need
Some Kind Of Sign) If We All Cry At
The Same Time Tonight

People Laugh When They're Feelin Sad
Someone Is Taking A Life, Hold On
Respect To Believe In Your Dreams
Tell Me Where Were You
When Your Children Cried Last Night?

Faces Fill With Madness
Miracles Unheard Of, Hold On
Faith Is Found In The Winds
All We Have To Do
Is Reach For The Truth

You Can Change The World (I Can't Do
It By Myself) You Can Touch The Sky
(Gonna Take Somebody's Help) You're
The Chosen One (I'm Gonna Need
Some Kind Of Sign) If We All Cry At
The Same Time Tonight

And When That Flag Blows
There'll Be No More Wars
And When All Calls
I Will Answer All Your Prayers
Prayers, Show The World

You Can Change The World (I Can't Do
It By Myself) You Can Touch The Sky
(Gonna Take Somebody's Help) You're
The Chosen One (I'm Gonna Need
Some Kind Of Sign) If We All Cry At
The Same Time Tonight
You Can Change The World You Can
Touch The Sky (Gonna Take Somebody's
Help) You're The Chosen One (I'm
Gonna Need Some Kind Of Sign)
If We All Cry At The Same Time Tonight
You Can Change The World
You Can Touch The Sky (Gonna Take
Somebody's Help) You're The chosen ONe
If we all cry at the same time tonight

Put It All On Me Why You Put All On Me

Change The World

INVINCIBLE

The Lost Children

We Pray For Our Fathers, Pray
For Our Mothers Wishing Our
Families Well We Sing Songs
For The Wishing, Of Those
Who Are Kissing But Not For
The Missing

So This One's For All The Lost
Children This One's For All The
Lost Children This One's For All
The Lost Children, Wishing Them
Well And Wishing Them Home

When You Sit There Addressing,
Counting Your Blessings Biding
Your Time When You Lay Me Down
Sleeping And My Heart Is Weeping
Because I'm Keeping A Place

For All The Lost Children This Is
For All The Lost Children This
One's For All The Lost Children,
Wishing Them Well And Wishing
Them Home

Home With Their Fathers,
Snug Close And Warm, Loving Their
Mothers I See The Door Simply Wide
Open But No One Can Find Thee

So Pray For All The Lost Children
This Is For All The Lost The Lost
Children This Is For All The Lost
The Lost Children Wishing Them
Well This Is For All The Lost The
Lost Children This One's For All
The Lost The Lost Children Just
Think Of All The Lost Children
Wishing Them Well, And Wishing
Them Home

Whatever Happens

He Gives Another Smile, Tries To
Understand Her Side To Show
That He Cares She Can't Stay In
The Room She's Consumed
With Everything That's Been Goin'
On She Says Whatever Happens,
Don't Let Go Of My Hand

Everything Will Be Alright, He
Assures Her But She Doesn't Hear
A Word That He Says Preoccupied,
She's Afraid Afraid What They Been
Doing Is Not Right He Doesn't Know
What To Say, So He Prays Whatever,
Whatever, Whatever

Whatever Happens, Don't Let Go Of
My Hand Whatever Happens, Don't
Let Go Of My Hand Whatever Happens,
Don't You Let Go Of My Hand

Don't Let Go Of My Hand
Don't Let Go Of My Hand

He's Working Day And Night, Thinks
He'll Make Her Happy Forgetting All
The Dreams That He Had He Doesn't
Realize It's Not The End Of The World
It Doesn't Have To Be That Bad She
Tries To Explain, "It's You That Makes
Me Happy," Whatever, Whatever,
Whatever

Whatever Happens, Don't Let Go Of
My Hand Whatever Happens, Don't
Let Go Of My Hand Whatever Happens,
Don't You Let Go Of My Hand

Whatever Happens, Don't Let Go Of
My Hand Whatever Happens, Don't
Let Go Of My Hand Whatever Happens,
Don't You Let Go Of My Hand

Whatever Happens, Don't Let Go Of
My Hand

Threatened

You're Fearing Me, 'Cause You Know
I'm A Beast Watching You When You
Sleep, When You're In Bed I'm
Underneath You're Trapped In Halls,
And My Face Is The Walls I'm The
Floor When You Fall, And When
You Scream It's 'Cause Of Me I'm
The Living Dead, The Dark Thoughts
In Your Head I Heard Just What You
Said That's Why You've Got To Be
Threatened By Me

(Chorus)
You Should Be Watching Me, You
Should Feel Threatened Why You
Sleep, Why You Creep, You Should
Be Threatened Every Time Your Lady
Speaks She Speaks To Me, Threatened
Half Of Me You'll Never Be, So You
Should Feel Threatened By Me

You Think You're By Yourself, But
It's My Touch You Felt I'm Not A
Ghost From Hell, But I've Got A
Spell On You Your Worst Nightmare,
It's Me, I'm Everywhere In One Blink
I'll Disappear, And Then I'll Come
Back To Haunt You I'm Telling You,
When You Lie Under A Tomb I'm
The One Watching You That's Why
You Got To Be Threatened By Me

You Should Be Watching Me, You
Should Feel Threatened Why You
Sleep, Why You Creep, You Should
Be Threatened Every Time Your Lady
Speaks She Speaks To Me, Threatened
Half Of Me You'll Never Be, So You
Should Feel Threatened By Me

(Rod Serling)
The Unknown Monster Is About To
Embark From A Far Corner, Out Of
The Dark A Nightmare, That's The
Case Never Neverland, That's The
Place This Particular Monster Can
Read Minds Be In Two Places At
The Same Time This Is Judgement
Night, Execution, Slaughter The
Devil, Ghosts, This Monster Is Torture
You Can Be Sure Of One Thing,
That's Fate A Human Presence That
You Feel Is Strange A Monster That
You Can See Disappear
A Monster, The Worst Thing To Fear.

(Chorus x3)

(Rod Serling)
What You Have Just Witnessed Could
Be The End Of A Particularly Terrifying
Nightmare. It Isn't. It's The Beginning.

Michael Jackson

Michael Jackson was not just the King of Pop he was the King of Charity. The 2000 Issue of the "Guinness Book Of Records" names Michael as the "Pop Star who supports the most charity organizations."

Michael also wrote "We Are The World" with Lionel Richie in 1985 and performed it as part of an all-star single to raise money for Africa in 1985. In 1986, he set up the "Michael Jackson United Negro College Fund Endowed Scholarship Fund". This $1.5 million fund is aimed towards students majoring in performance art and communications, with money given each year to students attending a UNCF member college or university.

He donated the proceeds from the sales of The Man In The Mirror to Camp Ronald McDonald for Good Times, a camp for children who suffer from cancer. Michael donated tickets to shows in is 1989 Bad Tour to underprivileged children. The proceeds from one of his shows in Los Angeles were donated to Childhelp USA, the biggest charity-organization against child-abuse. Childhelp of Southern California then established the "Michael Jackson International Institute for Research On Child Abuse".

In 1992, he established the Heal The World Foundation, whose work has included airlifting 6 tons of supplies to Sarajevo, instituting drug and alcohol abuse education and donating millions of dollars to less fortunate children. Whereas in 2004, The African Ambassadors' Spouses Association, honored Michael Jackson for his worldwide humanitarian efforts, due to his fiscal contribution of more than $50 million to various charities, including many organizations that feed the hungry in Africa.

The Humanitarian

The 39 known charities Michael Jackson supported:

AIDS Project L.A.
American Cancer Society
Angel Food
Big Brothers of Greater Los Angeles
BMI Foundation, Inc.
Brotherhood Crusade
Brothman Burn Center
Camp Ronald McDonald
Childhelp U.S.A.
Children's Institute International
Cities and Schools Scholarship Fund
Community Youth Sports & Arts Foundation
Congressional Black Caucus (CBC)
Dakar Foundation
Dreamstreet Kids
Dreams Come True Charity
Elizabeth Taylor Aids Foundation
Juvenile Diabetes Foundation
Love Match
Make-A-Wish Foundation
Minority Aids Project
Motown Museum
NAACP
National Rainbow Coalition
Rotary Club of Australia
Society of Singers
Starlight Foundation
The Carter Center's Atlanta Project
The Sickle Cell Research Foundation
Transafrica
United Negro College Fund (UNCF)
United Negro College Fund Ladder's of Hope
Volunteers of America
Watts Summer Festival
Wish Granting
YMCA - 28th Street/Crenshaw

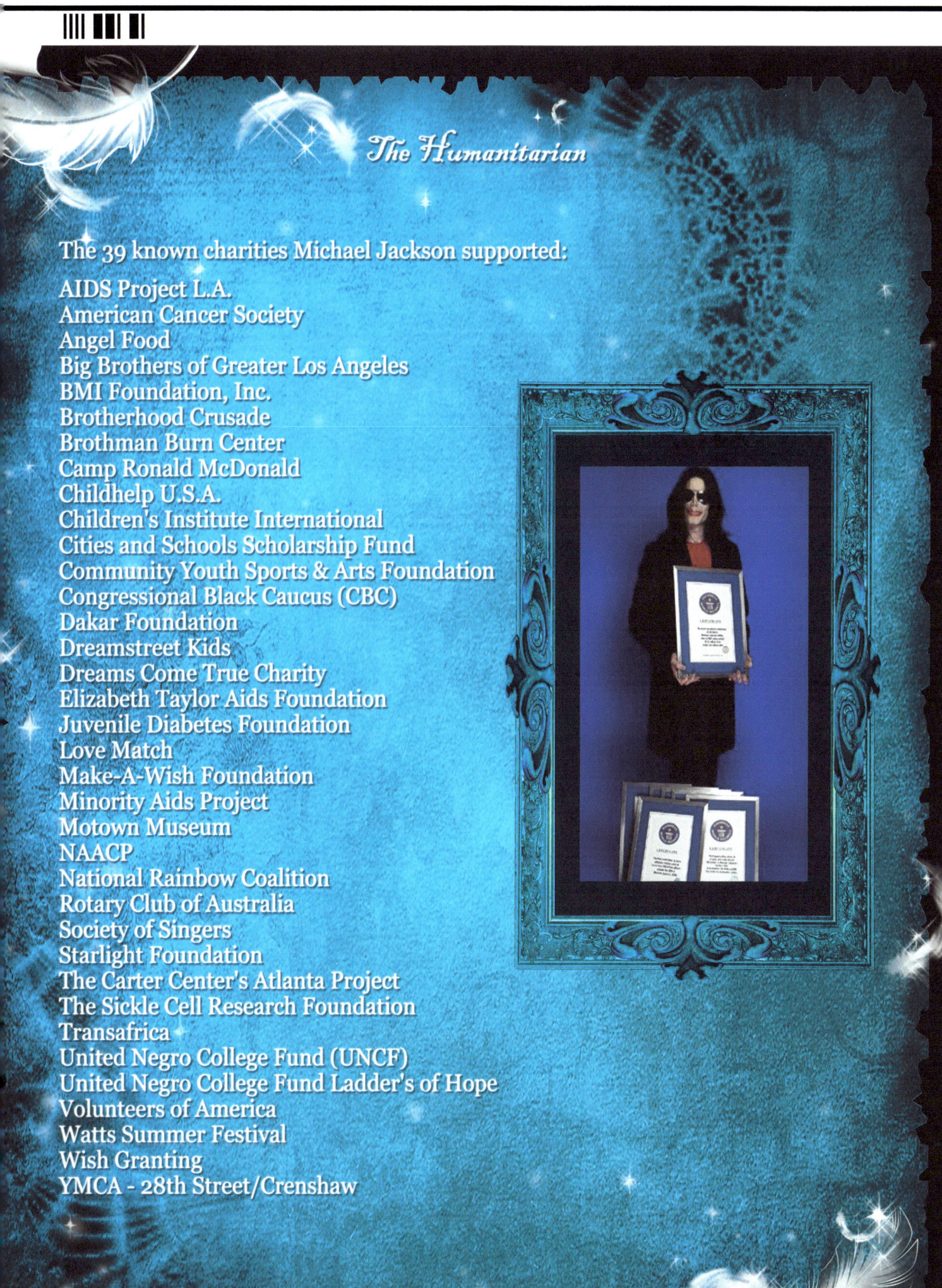

MICHAEL STYLE

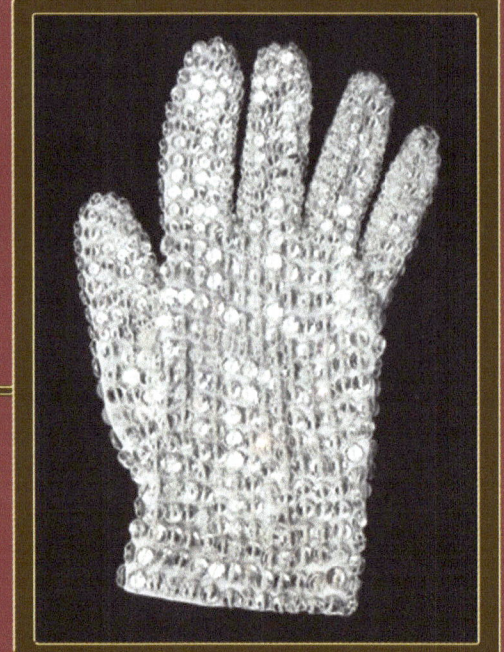

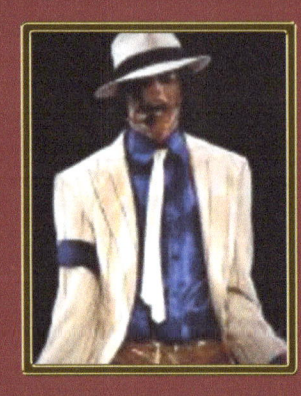

MICHAEL STYLE

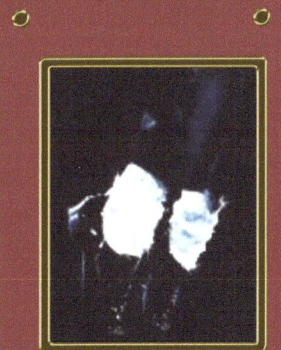

TRIVIA

Q. When was Michael Born?
A. August 29, 1958

Q. What day of the week was Michael born?
A. Friday

Q. What was the name of the street that the Jackson's lived on before they became famous?
A. Jackson Street

Q. What is Michael's middle name?
A. Joseph

Q. How many older siblings did Michael have?
A. Seven –Brandon Jackson (born March 12, 1957 - died at birth)

Q. How many sisters did Michael have?
A. Three

Q. What is the name of Michael's younger brother?
A. Steven Randall "Randy" Jackson

Q. Which of Michael's brothers shares a birthday with their mother?
A. Sigmund Esco Jackson "Jackie"

Q. What was the song Michael performed in his first grade program?
A. Climb Ev'ry Mountain

Q. Who was the first to recognize the Jackson's talent?
A. Their mother, Katherine Esther Scruse Jackson

Q. Where did the Jackson 5 perform their first complete show?
A. Mr. Lucky's Lounge

Q. When the Jackson 5 performed who stood to the right of Michael?
A. Jackie

Q. What year did the Jackson 5 win Amateur Night at the Apollo?
A. 1967

Q. What legendary singer saw them at Apollo and recommended them to Motown?
A. Gladys Knight

Q. What record label produced the Jackson 5 first studio album?
A. Steeltown

Q. What was the name of the Jackson 5's first single?
A. Big Boy

TRIVIA

Q. What year was "I Want You Back" released?
A. 1969

Q. How many singles were released off of Diana Ross Presents The Jackson 5?
A. One

Q. What are the names of the Jackson 5's first 4 #1 songs?
A. "I Want You Back", "ABC", "The Love You Save" and "I'll Be There"

Q. What were Michael's favorite 3 song while with the Jackson 5?
A. "Never Can Say Goodbye", I'll Be There" and "ABC"

Q. How many weeks did "I'll Be There" stay at #1?
A. Five

Q. The Jackson 5 made their first television appearance in August of 1969 at the Miss Black Pageant. What did they sing?
A. The Isley Brother's "It's Your Thing"

Q. What year did "Never Can Say Goodbye" released?
A. 1971

Q. The Jackson 5 cartoon show began in what year?
A. 1971

Q. How many seasons did the Jackson 5's cartoon air?
A. Two

Q. What was the name of Michael's first solo record?
A. Got To Be There

Q. In 1972 what movie did Michael sing the title song?
A. Ben

Q. What is the name of Michael's oldest sibling?
A. Maureen Reillette "Rebbie" Jackson Brown

Q. Which of Rebbie's songs was written and produced by Michael?
A. "Centipede"

Q. What 1984 hit song did Michael and Jermaine make guest appearances?
A. "Somebody's Watching Me" by Rockwell, who is Barry Gordy's son.

Q. What instrument did Michael play when he first joined the Jackson 5?
A. The congas

TRIVIA

Q. What was the name of the manager who joined the Jackson 5 team after they signed with Motown?
A. Suzanne de Passe

Q. What was the name of the movie that Michael made his film debut?
A. The Wiz

Q. What character did Michael play in The Wiz?
A. The Scarecrow

Q. On the set of The Wiz how did Michael Jackson embarrass Diana Ross?
A. By learning the dance steps quicker.

Q. During The Wiz time period why was Michael rushed to the hospital?
A. A blood vessel had burst in his lungs.

Q. What was the name of the Jackson's production company?
A. Peacock Production

Q. What was the name of Michael's first solo album after leaving his brothers?
A. Off The Wall

Q. Who produced the album Off The Wall?
A. Quincy Jones

Q. Where did Michael and Quincy Jones first meet?
A. On the set of The Wiz

Q. Which Off The Wall song did Randy play the percussions?
A. Don't Stop 'Til You Get Enough

Q. What song won Michael his first Grammy?
A. Don't Stop 'Til You Get Enough

Q. What was the first song Michael wrote?
A. Don't Stop 'Til You Get Enough

Q. Which Off The Wall song was a true story which Michael cried after performing?
A. She's Out Of My Life

Q. Which Academy Award Winning actress was Michael's first girlfriend?
A. Tatum O'Neal

Q. Where did Michael and Tatum go on their first date?
A. Hugh Hefner's Playboy Mansion

TRIVIA

Q. What album did Michael work on after Off The Wall?
A. Triumph, with his brothers

Q. What female vocalist recorded the scream at the beginning of Heartbreak Hotel?
A. Latoya Jackson

Q. Which professional magician did the special effect to allow Michael to disappear in a puff of smoke during the Triumph tour?
A. Doug Henning

Q. What category did Michael win his first Grammy?
A. Best R&B Vocal Performance

Q. What was the first single from the Thriller album?
A. The Girl Is Mine

Q. Who originally did the guitar solo in Beat It?
A. Eddie Van Halen

Q. Who wrote PYT (Pretty Young Thing) with Quincy Jones?
A. James Ingram

Q. Why did Quincy Jones want to name Billie Jean "Not My Lover"?
A. He thought people would think of tennis great Billie Jean King.

Q. Which two female artist sang backup on PYT?
A. Janet & Latoya Jackson

Q. What group wrote Human Nature?
A. Toto

Q. How many American Music Awards did Michael win from Off The Wall?
A. Three: Favorite Male Soul Artist, Favorite Soul Album & Favorite Soul Single for Don't Stop 'Til You Get Enough

Q. What was the name of the song Michael for Diana Ross?
A. Muscles

Q. What was the name of Michael's pet snake?
A. Muscles

Q. What year did Michael create the dance move the moonwalk?
A. He did not create the moonwalk but he did popularize it in when he preformed it in the 1983 Motown 25 Special

TRIVIA

Q. Why was Michael disappointed with his Motown 25 performance?
A. He didn't stay on his toes long enough after his big spin.

Q. Backstage after his Motown 25 performance what did his brothers do to him that they have never done?
A. Kissed Him

Q. Which film and Broadway stage dancer, called Michael after his Motown 25 performance and said "You're a hell of a mover, man"?
A. Fred Astaire

Q. Who did Michael give the jacket he wore in the Motown 25 special to?
A. Sammy Davis Jr.

Q. Why did Michael start wearing the single glove?
A. It was a fashion statement

Q. What Album did Michael win a Grammy for being the narrator?
A. E.T. The Extra Terrestrial

Q. What was the name of the song Michael sang for the E.T. soundtrack?
A. Someone In The Dark

Q. Which Jackson brother wanted their mother to make Michael stop wearing white socks?
A. Jermaine

Q. Why did Michael not like wearing jewelry?
A. It was a distraction

Q. What film director directed Thriller?
A. John Landis

Q. How many American Music Awards did Michael win from the album Thriller?
A. Eight: Special Award of Merit, Favorite Pop/Rock Album for Thriller, Favorite Soul/R&B Album for Thriller, Favorite Male Soul/R&B Vocalist, Favorite Pop/Rock Male Vocalist, Favorite Pop/Rock Single for "Billie Jean", Favorite Pop/Rock Video for Beat It, Favorite Soul/R&B Video for Beat It

Q. How many Grammys did Michael win from the album Thriller?
A. Seven: (He won one for Best Recording for Children for E.T.) Album of The Year for Thriller, Record of The Year for Beat It, Best Male Performance for Thriller, Producer of The Year for Thriller, Best Male Rock Vocal Performance for "Beat It, Best Male R&B Vocal Performance for Billie Jean, & Best New R&B Song for Billie Jean

Q. Michael holds The Guinness Book Of World Record for receiving the biggest commercial endorsement from what company?

TRIVIA

Q. What was the Victory Tour originally going to be called?
A. "The Final Curtain"

Q. Which Jackson brother did not participate in the Victory Tour?
A. All brothers participated.

Q. During the Victory Tour why would the wardrobe staff get annoyed with Michael?
A. He kept throwing his jackets into the audience.

Q. What did Michael do with the money he made from the Victory Tour?
A. Donated it to charities

Q. What was the name of the Disney short film that starred Michael?
A. Captain EO

Q. In what year was We Are The World recorded?
A. 1985

Q. Who wrote We Are The World with Michael?
A. Lionel Richie

Q. Who did Michael want to sing We Are The World?
A. Children

Q. What is the name of Michael's production company?
A. MJJ Productions

Q. What year did Michael write Moonwalk?
A. 1988

Q. Michael Jackson bought the Best Picture Oscar awarded to which film?
A. Citizen Kane

Q. What film did Michael record the song Childhood?
A. Free Willy 2

Q. What year did Michael perform at the Super Bowl?
A. In January 1993 Jackson performed during the halftime show at Super Bowl XXVII. It drew the largest viewing audience in the history of American television.

Q. How many number one singles did Michael Jackson have in his solo career?
A. Thirteen

TRIVIA

Q. Which Hollywood socialite was the Goddaughter of Michael?
A. Nicole Richie

Q. What year did Michael get is star on Hollywood Boulevard?
A. 1984

Q. Which President gave Michael an award for The Greatest of the Decade?
A. George H. Bush

Q. How many songs on the album Thriller, did Michael write?
A. Four: The Girl Is Mine, Beat It, Billie Jean & Wanna Be Startin' Somethin'

Q. In 2008 what famous fashion designer did Michael team up with to start his clothing line?
A. Christian Audigier

Q. In 1993 Michael received a patent for what item?
A. Michael and two partners by the U.S. Patent and Trade Office, patent No. 5,255,452 covers a "system for allowing a shoe wearer to lean forwardly beyond his center of gravity by virtue of wearing a specially designed pair of shoes."

 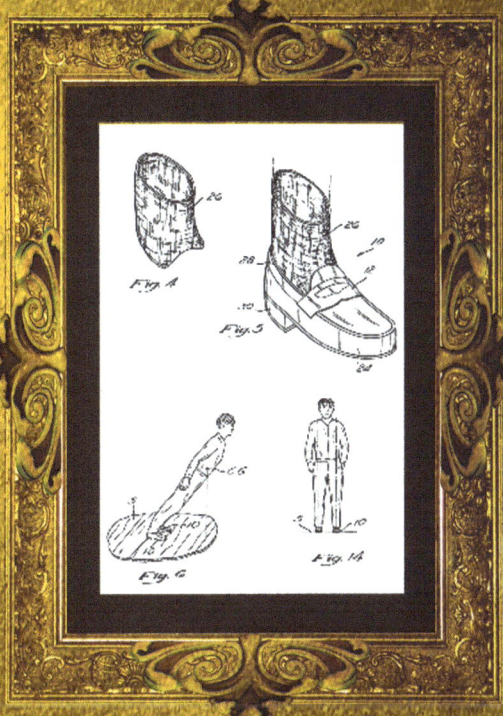

A heel slot in the shoes gets hitched to retractable pegs in a stage floor. Wearing the shoes, Jackson (or anyone) could seem to lean past his center of gravity without toppling. The effect would be most striking in live performances, during which harnesses and wires would be too cumbersome or impossible to disguise.

www.ingramcontent.com/pod-product-compliance